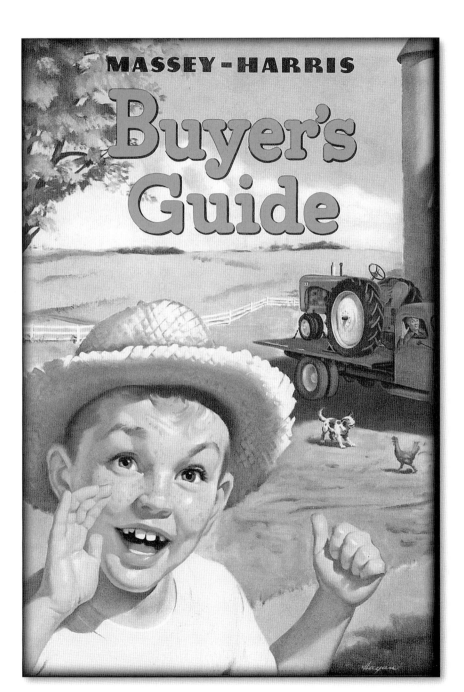

My First
TRACTOR

Stories of Farmers and Their First Love

With stories and artwork by

Michael Perry, Bob Artley, Roger Welsch, Bob Feller, Ben Logan, Gwen Petersen,

Ralph W. Sanders, Robert N. Pripps, Patricia Penton Leimbach, Randy Leffingwell,

Lee Klancher, Don Macmillan, Scott Garvey, John Dietz, and more

Foreword by Jerry Apps

Voyageur Press

Voyageur Press titles are also available at discounts in bulk quantity for industrial or sales-promotional use. For details write to Special Sales Manager at MBI Publishing Company, 400 First Avenue North, Suite 300, Minneapolis, MN 55401 USA.

To find out more about our books, visit us online at www.voyageurpress.com.

ISBN-13: 978-0-7603-3783-7

Editors: Amy Glaser and Michael Dregni

Design Manager: LeAnn Kuhlmann

Designed by: Elly Rochester

Cover designed by: Wendy Lutge

Printed in China

On the front cover and title page: Like grandfather, like grandson. Allen Martin sits on his 1935 John Deere Model B while his grandson, Jonathan Martin, pilots a Model 60 pedal tractor. *Keith Baum*

On the contents page 5: Junior proudly refuels the family Farmall. *Library of Congress*

On the contents page 6: Top: Case brochure painting with Grandad and Pa showing their boys the workings of the Case steamer. Bottom: Sis learns to plow with the family's new Ford-Ferguson 9N.

On the back cover: Bob Feller and his Caterpillar. *Ralph Sanders. Memories of a Former Kid* by artist Bob Artley.

On the frontispiece: The arrival of the new tractor on the farm: a painting from the front cover of Massey-Harris' mid-1950s *Buyer's Guide.*

CONTENTS

FOREWORD

My First Tractor

BY JERRY APPS

In 1945, a couple months after the end of World War II, Dad bought a new 1943 Farmall H tractor. I remember that fall day when the dealer unloaded the H and said, "I think you'll like it." Dad paid $1,750 for his new tractor, which was a considerable amount of money at the time. It was red, it was shiny, and it had big 11-inch x 38-inch tires in the back and front tires close together in the front. A row-crop model. It came with a two-row cultivator that hung on each side. Alas, it did not have a hydraulic system so lifting and lowering the cultivator was more than a challenge for a kid my size. The Farmall did have a power take-off and a belt pulley. And interestingly, it had been built with steel wheels, those in the back with lugs that dug into the ground providing traction. The dealer's very skilled welder had removed the steel and attached rims for rubber tires, no small task. He had done an excellent job, for even when driving down our country road in fifth gear there was no wobble or wiggle.

Like a first child in a family, a farmer's first tractor marked a turning point in his life. When our first tractor rolled off the delivery truck and stood shining under the big elm tree in front of our farm house everything changed. Whether we were aware of it or not, our new tractor marked the beginning of what some agricultural historians call the second revolution in agriculture.

For thousands of years, farmers worked the land by hand. They stirred the soil with primitive, often wooden, soil breaking equipment. They scattered the seeds by hand and trusted nature to do the rest. The days were long and the work backbreaking. The crops they harvested were often meager and insufficient and in bad years people starved. As the years passed, farmers then, as now, searched for ways of making the work easier and the harvest greater.

Farmers discovered that hitching an animal to the groundbreaking implement, a plow, made stirring the soil many times easier. Fixing a piece of metal to the digging end of the plow allowed for deeper digging and an implement that was immediately sturdier and longer lasting.

The first revolution in agriculture came into its own when much of the hand labor of farming, the work requiring brute strength, was taken over by animals. In the United States, in the 1700s to the mid-1800s, oxen pulled the plows, toted the heavy wagons, pulled logs from the forests, and transported farm families to the villages for supplies. Oxen were strong, dependable, and easily obtainable—you could grow your own—but they were so slow. It's said that if you drove your family to Sunday church with an ox cart, you must start out on Friday to arrive on time.

During the early 1800s, new types of farm machinery began appearing. Many of these early inventors were farmers and/or blacksmiths. Great progress was made in inventing everything from grain drills to manure spreaders, from threshing machines to grain binders, and even new types of plows. Farmers in the Midwest quickly discovered that the plows they had brought with them from New England, many of them constructed of cast iron, did not work well in heavier Midwestern soils. In 1833, John Lane arrived in Illinois from New England and began experimenting with a plow that would turn Midwestern soil. He discovered that a tempered steel moldboard was the answer.

John Deere came to Illinois from Vermont in 1836 and opened a blacksmith shop where he shoed horses, fixed wagon wheels, and heard farmers complain about their plows. He apparently didn't know about John Lane's plow as he took an old saw blade, cut off the teeth, and formed it into a moldboard for a plow. His new plow quickly caught on. In 1848, Deere moved his business to Moline, Illinois, and built a new factory with capacity of producing 4,000 plows annually.

In the mid-1800s, the Midwest emerged as a wheat growing center. Ohio, Indiana, Illinois, Wisconsin, and Iowa led the nation in wheat production. During the Civil War, 1861, Illinois led all the states in the production of wheat with Wisconsin in second place. Many of these wheat farmers worked new ground, broke it with teams of oxen, sometimes six or eight of the brutes strung out in a line with a man hanging onto the handles of a breaking plow that lurched through the heavy sod. Beyond breaking the soil, wheat growing was essentially hand work. Farmers scattered the wheat kernels by hand. They cut the wheat with a cradle, gathered it and bound it into bundles by hand, and stood the bundles into shocks to dry. When dry, these wheat farmers, some planting and harvesting twenty acres and more, hauled their crop to the barn where the wheat kernels were separated from the straw on the threshing floor using a flail, or allowing the oxen to walk on the wheat. It was slow, tedious, and hard work, from planting to harvesting.

Cyrus McCormick was one of the notable inventors of the day. A Virginia farmer and son of a farmer-blacksmith, he experimented with machines that could cut grain. He patented his famous McCormick reaper in 1834, but sales were slow. The first problem for McCormick was the machine's price. In 1849, the price of a McCormick reaper was $130.00 with additional freight charges. A price of a new grain cradle was about $2.00. Secondly, McCormick's reaper required a sturdy team of draft horses; many farmers still depended on oxen as their power source.

Starting in the 1830s, horse dealers began importing the larger draft horse breeds from Europe—Percherons, Belgians, and Clydesdales especially, but other breeds as well. The Midwestern soils, heavier and more difficult to work than the thinner soils of New England, required more power for plowing and other basic field work—and these horses could pull the newfangled reapers as well. But farmers, then as now, were slow to change.

With the Civil War, they were forced to do things differently. Thousands of men marched off to war and the farm women, children, and old men were left to harvest the crops, especially the enormous wheat crops.

There were not enough men available to do the cradling, shocking, and hand threshing. McCormick reaper salesmen were quick to step forward with the solution to the problem—purchase a reaper.

Meanwhile, inventors like J. I. Case of Racine had perfected a mechanical threshing machine to replace the flailing and animals walking on the grain to thresh it. By the 1860s, the horse-powered Case threshing machine (there were other manufacturers, too) had become popular. In the late 1800s, steam traction engines—the forerunner of today's farm tractor—began appearing. Although huge, these ponderous beasts with steel wheels and a cast iron frame, not too different from a small steam locomotive, could be driven down the road toting a threshing machine behind. By 1886, J. I. Case had become the premier manufacturer of steam engines in the world.

In the early 1900s, horse-drawn farm equipment had become standard on farms throughout the country. The steam powered tractors, occasionally found their way into farmer's fields, pulling plows and such, but they were such clumsy and heavy beasts that most farmers did not use them. From 1900 to 1910, the number of draft horses in the United States increased from 13 million to 23 million. In 1919 U.S. horse numbers reached an all time high, nearly 26 million.

With the development of gasoline-powered internal combustion engines, tractors began slowly appearing on the nation's farms. But through the long years of the Great Depression, 1929–1941, thousands of farmers continued farming with their trusty draft horse teams. Many farmers simply couldn't afford one of these newfangled tractors that they saw at county fairs and occasionally in their home communities.

That was the case on my home farm in central Wisconsin. We farmed all through the Depression years with horses. When farm prices came up a bit during World War II (1941–1945), my dad had some extra money for a tractor, but essentially no tractors were available. All the major manufacturers, McCormick, which had become McCormick Deering and then International Harvester, J. I. Case, Allis-Chalmers, John Deere, Ford, and others were making products for the war effort.

Frank, Charlie, and Dick, our trusty work horses, continued on through the war. Our farming practices had changed little from what my grandfather had done. But my dad had his mind set for a tractor. Our very first tractor was home-made. Calling it a tractor was a bit of a stretch, especially when it was compared with the factory-made models, Dad worked with Jim Colligan, a blacksmith and welder in Wild Rose, Wisconsin. Together, they designed a tractor based on a stripped down Ford truck. Colligan shortened the frame, but kept the engine and the power train. He used discarded county snowplow tires in back and kept the original truck tires in front. He painted the whole thing with aluminum colored paint. The transmission had four speeds, but we only used what was called dual-low, the lowest, most powerful speed.

It had enough power and traction (with chains on the back wheels) to pull two 14-inch plows. The machine would pull a wagon of course, and it was wonderful for going for the cows in the far pasture of the farm. When Dad wasn't around, I would slip the transmission into second and sometimes even in third, and the old Ford with the over-sized tires in the back would go like the wind.

But there were many tasks the home-made Ford tractor could not do. It couldn't cultivate corn or potatoes. It did not have a pulley for a drive belt, nor did it have a power take-off. And it had but one working speed. Even though this old home-made machine had many shortcomings, it gave us a taste of the future; an inkling of what it would be like to farm with a tractor and leave the horses in the pasture. An entry way into what became the second revolution in agriculture.

Dad sold the old home-made Ford tractor and now the new red H stood in its place, waiting for spring work. We used the H for light jobs around the farm that late autumn for most of the fall work had been completed, the threshing done, the silo filled, and the corn harvested. Our draft horses stayed in the pasture. Dad had no intention of selling them as he was not yet completely sold on the virtues of a tractor, having spent most of his life driving horses. His favorite saying in those days, when asked why he kept his team, "No matter how cold it is, the horses will always start."

I remember winter days when the old home-made Ford tractor wouldn't start and we hitched the team to the front of it and dragged it around the yard until it did. Dad figured the same would be true for the Farmall H, but, I don't remember a day in winter when it didn't start. It had a six-volt system with magneto, which provided a hot spark—learned the hard way by those who held onto a wire to see if things were working while the engine was cranked.

Dad did shorten the tongues on several pieces of horse-drawn equipment such as the grain binder, corn binder, and hay wagon so they could be pulled behind the tractor.

The same fall that dad bought the red Farmall, our nearest neighbor, Bill Miller, bought a spanking new green John Deere B. From that day forward, as long as these old neighbors farmed, the friendly competition between red and green never stopped. Those old enough to remember will recall that the Farmall had a four-cylinder engine. International Harvester, the Farmall manufacturer, claimed the drawbar horsepower at 19, belt horsepower at 24, and power take-off at 29. Our H had an electric starter, a foot clutch, and a foot brake for each rear wheel.

Bill Miller's John Deere B was a bit more powerful with a drawbar HP of 24, belt HP at 27, and PTO at 22. It was two-cylinder, had a hand clutch, and you started it by turning a big cast-iron flywheel. This detailed horsepower information is important because Bill never let my dad forget that his was the more powerful of the two machines and could do tasks our H could not.

In those days, (mid-1940s–1950s) farmers in our neighborhood still cut grain with binders, shocked the bundles, and then threshed the grain with a threshing machine that made the rounds of the neighborhood with all the neighbors helping out. The big test came during the summer of 1946 when Dad and Bill Miller bought a threshing machine, each owning a half-share. The intent was that they would thresh each other's grain and then thresh the other farmers in the neighborhood. The question was which tractor, the Farmall H or the John Deere B would power the 22-inch Case threshing machine. As threshing machines go, a 22-incher is on the small side, so either tractor had the potential for doing the job. On paper at least, the John Deere ought to out perform the Farmall—and that's what Bill Miller let my dad know.

They did a practice run at our farm, without any grain. Bill backed his B into the belt, engaged the pulley, and slowly the threshing machine came to life, the John Deere popping merrily along and Bill smiling like he'd won the day. Then Dad backed the Farmall into position and the same thing happened. The threshing machine came to life, the H motored along with little challenge, and for the moment the two old friends declared a draw. They decided that they would take turns, one day the H would power the thresher, the next day the B.

The real test came a couple days later when we threshed grain at our farm. Bill backed his B into the belt and eased the hand throttle forward. The B popped loudly a couple of times, the threshing machine shuddered and its many belts and chains began turning this way and that, awaiting the first oat bundles.

George Kolka, on the bundle wagon, waited for Bill's signal to start tossing bundles into the machine. Bill slowly increased the speed of the threshing machine and nodded his head to George, who began tossing in oat bundles, one after the other, straight and true as a good bundle pitcher will do. The John Deere protested a bit and popped more loudly with the increasingly challenge from the working machine. George, well aware of the competition going on between Bill and my dad, was smiling as he kept tossing bundles into the thresher. The B popped ever louder, and then the main drive belt, the one that runs from the tractor to the thresher began snapping up and down. George kept tossing bundles, the B popped even louder and the snapping became more severe. Bill, with the saddest look on his face I had ever seen, signaled for George to stop.

"Back your H into the belt," Bill said. "Something's not right with my B today."

Smiling but not saying anything, Dad backed the Farmall H into position and the threshing continued without a hitch. From that day forward, tractor discussions in our neighborhood almost always turned to the day that the poppin' Johnnie was outdone by a Farmall H, and of the values of a four-cylinder machine over a two-cylinder machine when it came to belt work.

Aside from the labor saved and the friendly farmer competition, the arrival of the first tractor marked the end of an era and the beginning of a new one. Horse-drawn farming was replaced with tractor farming, and the changes were much more profound than most realized. Combines replaced grain binders and threshing machines—and the community threshing crews. Corn pickers and then corn combines replaced corn binders, corn shocks, and corn shredder bees. Farms became larger as tractors made work easier. And young people began leaving the farms for the cities as farm numbers declined and continue to do so. Entire communities changed, villages lost population, churches closed, schools consolidated. The coming of the tractor, along with electricity, television, and a host of other "modern" conveniences marked the beginning of a new era in agriculture.

Every Child Wants a Tractor

Junior drops his toy Farmall as he catches sight of the family's new arrival in this painting from a 1950s International Harvester calendar.

27 In. Long

$1.00
POSTPAID

4 In Set 1

Your Play Farm Is Not Complete Without This 4-in-1 Tractor Set

Every child loves to play with a Tractor Set. We offer four pieces for only $1.00, **Postpaid**. Our biggest seller in a mechanical toy and one of our best values. Fits the wants of every child, because of its wonderful construction and play value. Just imagine the fun the kiddies will have hitching the different pieces behind the tractor to do the different jobs around your farm, just like Dad does with his big tractor. Our set consists of: Tractor with man driver, a four-wheel wagon, two-wheel rake and disc harrow. Tractor has strong spring motor. When all pieces are hooked together set measures 27 inches long over all. **Tractor is 7⅞ inches long,** other three pieces in proportion. Made of lithographed metal and has strong spring motor.
49T5748—Postpaid....... **$1.00**

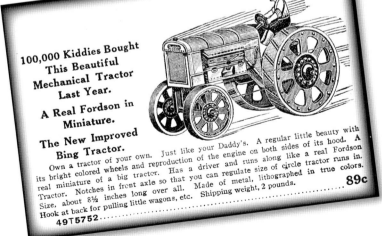

89c

100,000 Kiddies Bought This Beautiful Mechanical Tractor Last Year.

A Real Fordson in Miniature.

The New Improved Bing Tractor.

Own a tractor of your own. Just like your Daddy's. A regular little beauty with its bright colored wheels and reproduction of the engine on both sides of its hood. A real miniature of a big tractor. Has a driver and runs along like a real Fordson Tractor. Notches in front axle so that you can regulate size of circle tractor runs in. Size, about 8½ inches long over all. Made of metal, lithographed in true colors. Hook at back for pulling little wagons, etc. Shipping weight, 2 pounds. **89c**
49T5752..........

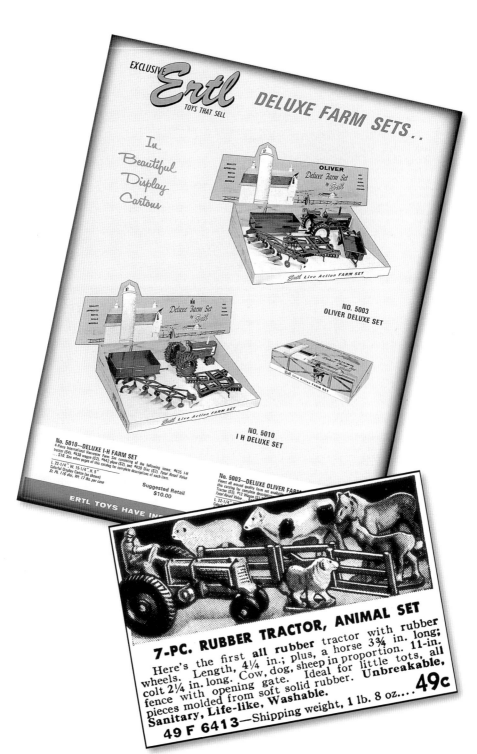

EXCLUSIVE *Ertl* DELUXE FARM SETS...

TOYS THAT SELL

In Beautiful Display Cartons

QUALITY APPROVED METAL SCALE MODELS

OLIVER Deluxe Farm Set by *Ertl*

Ertl Live Action FARM SET

Deluxe Farm Set by *Ertl*

QUALITY APPROVED METAL SCALE MODELS

Ertl Live Action FARM SET

NO. 5010
I H DELUXE SET

NO. 5003
OLIVER DELUXE SET

Ertl Live Action FARM SET

No. 5010—DELUXE I-H FARM SET
4-Piece International Harvester Farm Set consisting of the following items: #435 I-H Tractor ($4), #438 wagon ($2), #645 plow ($2), and #438 Disc ($2). Total Retail Value ...$10. See other pages of this catalog for complete descriptions of each item.
L. 22-1/4". W. 15-1/4". H. 5"
Colorful Display Carton (as shown)
St. Pk. 1/6 doz. Wt. 17 lbs. per case

Suggested Retail
$10.00

No. 5003—DELUXE OLIVER FARM
Finest all around quality farm set available ... this catalog for complete description ... Tractor ($3), #12 Wagon ($ ...
Total Retail Value ... $ ...
L. 22-1/4" W. ...
Colorful ...

ERTL TOYS HAVE IN...

Guaranteed Steam Engines

Read This! These beautifully finished Toy Engines are real quality and are such clever imitations of large engines, even in small details, that they take the eye of every boy.

Boys! This Is a Crackerjack Engine. Has Governor, Water Glass and Everything.

Just think, the double piston works from a real steam cylinder; dummy governor actually revolves. Has steam dome, safety valve, brass encased glass water gauge and whistle that blows loud enough for any boy. Big flywheel with pulley for running toys. Polished spun brass boiler. Painted cast iron base, 5¾x6 inches. Height over all, 5¾ inches. Shipping weight, 4⅝ pounds.

Large Size.
49N5330........ **$3.98**

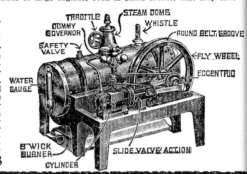

THROTTLE

STEAM DOME

DUMMY GOVERNOR

WHISTLE

ROUND BELT GROOVE

SAFETY VALVE

FLY WHEEL

WATER GAUGE

ECCENTRIC

6 WICK BURNER

SLIDE VALVE ACTION

CYLINDER

Steam Tractors.

Just Like Dad's. They Move Under Their Own Power in Circle or Straight.

Our Finest Toy Tractor.
Accurate in detail and proportion. Brass boiler, handsome gunmetal finish. Flywheel has nickeled face. Chain drive. Boiler has wood handle drain cock, oil cup and safety valve. Alcohol burner; also _____ full direct _____ in. long. _____
49N53 _____

Medium Size Tractor.
Runs in a circle or straight. Spun brass boiler; alcohol lamp. Steam cylinder and pistons. Whistle. _____

Steam Roller That Reverses.
Runs forward or backward. Spun brass boiler, whistle and reverse lever. _____ belt. Cab for _____, 6¾ inches; _____ hes. Alcohol _____ ping weight, _____

$4.67

Young Love

BY ROGER WELSCH

Roger Welsch is a farm tractor poet, philosopher, and paleontologist all rolled into one.

He is also a high priest of the vintage tractor world, spreading the good word about tractors far and wide. During his stint as a television personality on CBS TV's *Sunday Morning* program, Roger showcased tractors whenever he could. His writings on farm tractors have appeared in magazines everywhere from *Successful Farming* and *Nebraska Farmer* to *Esquire* and *Smithsonian*. In addition, he is the author of more than twenty books, including several on the trials and tribulations of living with tractors, including *Old Tractors and the Men Who Love Them* and *Busted Tractors and Rusty Knuckles*. As John Carter of the Nebraska State Historical Society noted, "We all knew sooner or later that Roger would write a book about religion."

He lives on a farm in the middle of Nebraska with his collection of Allis-Chalmers machines.

"Young love, first love, Filled with true devotion—
Young love, our love. We share with deep emotion…."
—Sonny James, "Young Love," 1957

A few weeks ago we got a curious telephone call left on our answering service. The caller said he runs a small shop in Lincoln, about 120 miles east of here and where I grew up. He had recently bought a box of junque [sic] at a sale and while going through it he found a little tattered book…a diary. After thumbing through it a bit and connecting some obscure, faded, potentially embarrassing dots he deduced that it had been in fact my diary. From 1953 to 1955, when I was in high school. He wondered if I wanted it, making a point that it was juicy material for blackmailing if that's the route I preferred…citing one entry from 1953, "Tomorrow for sure I am going to kiss Peggy."

That wouldn't be all that embarrassing if I didn't have vague memories of what happened on that occasion. Or more precisely what didn't happen on that occasion. I didn't kiss Peggy. In fact, as my ancient narrative continued I made other, similar promises to myself. As I turned the faded, battered pages (all the while wondering where the heck that diary had been for the last 55 years) I was reminded with considerable discomfort that I also had not kissed Millicent. Or Harriett. Or Karen, Jan, Kay, or Myrna. Or anyone.

I came to romance late in my life. It's just a good thing (for me) that I got an earlier, if belated, start with women than I did with tractors. But even in my eventual, deep affection for old tractors I was slow to warm, as it were, to the occasion.

When I was in the haying fields of eastern Wyoming with my Uncle Fred, Cousin Dick and I rode the workhorses pulling the hay derrick up to tip hay onto the top of the stack. Then we got up on that stack and stomped it down, carrying the itchies with us for many days to come. There were tractors involved in the haying process, one turned around to run in reverse and serve as a sweep to bring hay to the derrick but I was busy with horses and horsing around, paid no attention to roaring machines and have little memory of them, not even what make Uncle Fred preferred.

My Uncle Sam, just a few miles to the north near Lingle, had (I remember) quite a number of tractors…each with a piece of equipment permanently bolted to it so he never had to worry about the hazards that accompanied mounting and dismounting ag equipment. I have no idea what kind of tractors Uncle Sam had. Again I had no interest in such matters.

My first real impression of a tractor worthy of admiration and/or curiosity did make a dent in my psyche. That would have been about 1967 or maybe 1968. I was invited over for a chat with the notable, admirable, amazing John G. Neihardt, a Nebraska literary giant. I was probably still glassy-eyed about having been in the presence of that luminary a couple hours later when Julius Young, at whose home in Lincoln Neihardt lived for some years, showed me out of the Youngs' elegant home, but as we headed toward my car, he said he wanted to show me something… his pride and joy. Something really special. Having John Neihardt in residence in your living room isn't special enough?! What could be more special than that, I wondered.

We waded through some tall weeds to the rear of an outbuilding of his property in urban Lincoln, but large and isolated enough to count as rural. He kicked down some of the weeds and pulled a tarp off of a small, low, mysterious machine. A tractor. But a tractor that even I in my complete disregard for any machinery, yet tractors, realized was indeed something remarkable. I did not at that time know the name, make, or model of a single tractor. But I remember that spidery little beast as if it were yesterday. It was an Allis-Chalmers. An Allis-Chalmers G. As impressed as I was by this curious machine, it never occurred to me that I would ever own an Allis-Chalmers G model tractor, or for that matter any tractor at all. That idea simply was not in my realm of imagination or inclination. But I sure as heck never forgot what I saw behind Julius Young's shed and what the name of that remarkable and exotic machine was. Perhaps that was the first glimmer of a romance that was to bloom eventually into a full fledged TLC (Tractor Love Complex).

In 1974 I bought this sand and gravel pile I call a tree farm. Although I certainly had never entertained the notion of having a tractor, the unrecognized need was apparently tattooed across my forehead because a neighbor across the street, when I mentioned that I had acquired some land, asked me what I had for a tractor. Uuuuuh… tractor? What would I do with a tractor? "Well, jeez, Rog, you have to have a tractor!"

Maybe it was just a hustle. He said his father had an old John Deere B that ran just fine…the kind you start by spinning the flywheel. I had no idea what he was talking about but it sounded pretty crazy to me. Maybe he was just kidding. "He'd let you have it for a hundred dollars," my neighbor said. Well, I may have been a city boy but I was no idiot! No way was I going to throw away $100 on an old tractor! Nosirreebob! Besides, who was going to drive that thing 150 miles to my farm?! I may have been born on a Saturday, but it wasn't last Saturday! And that's how close I came to being a Greenie.

I can't be sure of the timing but it was just a couple years later that another friend…mysteriously living just across the same street and right behind the guy who offered me the Deere…asked me much the same question: "How can you have a 'farm' and not have a tractor?" To him the very thought was just as absurd as the notion of having a tractor still seemed to me. I stood stupid. "Look," he said sternly. "I have an old tractor sitting in a wood lot on a farm just south of here. I haven't used it for a year or so and can't imagine that I will be needing it, so if you want it, you can have it."

I didn't have the heart to tell him I didn't need it either, or want it. Me having a tractor would have been for all the world like the dog that finally catches up with the UPS delivery truck. What was I supposed to do with it now that I had it? Not a clue… But it began to seem obvious that the Great Mysteries of the Universe had in mind for me to have a tractor. So I said, uh, okay. And I found a farmer friend who had a trailer and lived near the farm with the woodlot. In fact, he knew the guy who had originally owned that tractor (and I mean or-dang-iginally, and in fact he knew that very tractor by name). He said you bet, he would help me haul that machine out here.

Do I remember that day? Did Bernadette Soubirous remember the day of her vision at Lourdes?! Jeez, I can remember the crunch of my boots hitting the dusty ground in the drive of that farm. I remember the first flash of orange from the woodlot. I recall the sensation of the stinging nettles brushing against my bare arms as I made my way through the jungle to get to the tractor. I can still taste the excitement…and the crushing, bitter dismay when I got close enough to the "tractor" to realize I'd been had. The machine was buried in sticks, leaves, and weeds.

It obviously hadn't been started for years. It was nothing but a tangle of rusting junk.

My friend with the trailer had another opinion: "She's a beauty, Rog. An Allis WC. A classic. And the tires are still up!" He took the crank hanging on a wire by the seat and tested the crankshaft. "Look at that, Rog! The engine's free!" Oh boy. Thrill thrill.

We hooked a winch to the wreck, cut down some trees and brush, and started to drag the hulk out into the yard and toward the trailer. "Hey, Rog, I have an idea. Let's put some gas in her and see if maybe we can't drive her up onto the trailer." Yeah sure…why don't we pray for divine intervention and hope that a band of angels comes down and just levitates that thing up the ramps?! Sopped in sweat and pessimism, I watched him pour a pint or two of gasoline into the tank, set the choke, and turn the crank.

I couldn't believe what happened next—that tractor coughed…or at least I think it coughed. My friend straightened up and stepped back, grinning like an idiot. Again he approached the machine, fitted the crank to the shaft and gave it another twist.

An enormous roar (a sound that has pretty much rendered me deaf in the intervening 40 years) staggered me into slack-jawed amazement. I was buried in a cloud of dirt, leaves, sticks, mouse poop, and now a few mice blowing out from under the tractor's sheet metal. Now I was the one with the stupid grin on my face. I simply couldn't believe it. Not just that the tractor started and was running…but that I was suddenly, totally, and inexplicably in love. Just like that, I had become an Allis-Chalmers man, forsaking all others green, yellow, gray, or red forever. My friend waved me grandly up onto the seat, in part because any other form of communication was impossible in the flying debris and deafening roar. Good grief, I didn't even know how to get onto a tractor, yet drive one! But I clambered up onto the iron seat. I got Sweet Allis…as she was instantly dubbed…into some gear or another with great grinding and gnashing of its and my teeth, and I eased out the clutch.

If I could have I would have called my mother! "Mom! I'm driving a tractor!" I got her (the tractor, not Mom) up onto the trailer without falling off and dying, and my friend hit the killer switch before we burned up the engine, that possibly was running with no oil or coolant in the block. I wish I had a photo of my face on the long haul across Nebraska to my farm with that tractor. I must have been grinning like an idiot. Like right after the entry in my diary when I had finally managed to plant a kiss on Barbara (last name omitted to protect her dignity in case her grandchildren read tractor books like this).

For ten more years Sweet Allis slept here on this place of ours with only a mulberry tree and a tarp for protection, starting every single time I turned the crank, summer and winter, blazing heat, or roaring blizzard. On many occasions when not a single other of a dozen modern, fancy, expensive vehicles on this place would start, I could count on Sweet Allis. She never let me down.

It's been some months since she's roared her roar for me now. Even though she still stands ready, as proud and pretty as she was all those years before, I am not. Even though she is exactly as old as I am, born in the same year...1936.

I didn't know it at the time or for many years to come but that good ol' girl changed my life. No kidding. A tractor...changed my life. I grew up not simply with a lack of interest in mechanicking [sic] but with a genuine antipathy toward the very notions of bruised knuckles, greasy fingernails, and a disposition founded on imponderables like stuck pistons, twisted off bolts, and shredded gears. So, for ten years I took Sweet Allis into town and had Service Station Mel do any servicing she needed. The tool I owned was a bad pair of pliers. Maybe a screwdriver somewhere, if I could find it, usually with the intent of using it as a wood chisel. But one day, for reasons I no longer remember nor can imagine, I decided to change her oil myself. I had a rough idea of where the oil sump was...and that's about all I knew. I had no building to work in and couldn't even call myself a shade-tree mechanic because we still didn't have any trees at the house big enough to throw down shade. So I crawled under my orange beauty with those pliers and tried to turn out the drain plug. It wouldn't budge. I tried harder...and started to round off the corners on the plug, which even I knew wasn't a good idea. Then I went to Mel and asked for advice. "Mel, how do I get that drain plug out of the oil pan?" I said, summoning up all the mechanical sophistication I had. And Mel gave me a quick lesson in the basics of breaking loose stuck parts, pretty much the heart of all antique tractor mechanicking. "Use plenty of a good penetrating oil," he said. "Here...take this can. There's enough left in there to pretty much do the job. Get yourself a real open end wrench that fits that plug. Try turning it in a touch first, and then apply some pressure to turn it out. Tap it lightly with a hammer, straight on, which may jar loose the threads. Then tap it while applying some pressure on your wrench. If that doesn't work, bring her up here and we'll see what we can do."

Oh man…this just didn't sound like any fun at all. But I did as I was told, what with being 100 percent German and all. Squirt penetrating oil. Apply pressure to tighten plug, and then lightly to back the plug out. Nothing. Tap tap tap with the hammer. Nothing. More penetrant. Tap tap tap while applying pressure and…did that thing just move or was it my imagination? No! It moved. I turned it in a sixteen or twentieth of a turn. Yes, it was moving in the pan threads! I turned it back out and…wow…now it turned easily. I grabbed an old bucket and lay there in ecstasy as the black, heavy oil splashed into the bucket and into my hair. I had done it. I was, by golly, a mechanic.

Hey, if I managed to get that done, I began to wonder if I could just maybe do something about the left brake that never quite worked, the lever pulling too far back and stopping before ever tightening the pad, belt, chain, disc, or whatever lay under the cast iron cover that held the brake lever and was fastened to the frame with two bolts. I bought another wrench. My mechanicking career might have ended right then and there, I suppose, if those bolts had been rusted into place, but they weren't. They turned out easily, and I lifted the iron cover on the brake compartment. I peered into the dark hole and fished out the spider webs with a stick. And there it was…a device so simple that even a complete idiot—which is to say, me—could see how this system worked. And there was a long bolt across the end of the belt around the axle that was obviously a way to adjust the brake. I turned it. I put the brake mechanism cap back on loosely and pulled at the brake lever and… I couldn't believe it. This worked too! I had now not just broken loose a stuck oil plug but I had actually repaired a defective brake. No, I hadn't replaced any broken or worn parts and no, I hadn't actually gone beyond the most superficial of Sweet Allis' more intimate parts but the fuse had been lit. Not just for tractor work but for the real purpose of most antique tractor restoration…an excuse to buy more tools. And buy I did. I spent years poring over tool catalogs, parts lists, service and repair manuals, and shop guides. Just as I had come late to the art and delight of kissing, at the age of 50+ I had been bitten by the bug of tractor mechanicking, and I owed it all...well, not the kissing part...to Sweet Allis.

I don't want to get all mushy here. That's not my style. (Ask Lovely Linda!) And don't get me wrong, I love my AGCO ST47a...she's orange!...and she is one shiny, pretty young thing. Less than 100 hours on her. The AGCO is the most expensive vehicle I have ever owned in my life, and worth every cent she cost me. But right there beside her in the machine rests my first love, Sweet Allis...just as pretty if faded, just as beloved if not quite as fancy, just as wonderful if not quite as useful. And she didn't cost me a dime.

Nah...that thing? Just another tractor. An old beater. A friend gave her to me some years ago. Oh yeah, we've had some good times together, but now I use the big ACGO A-GoGo for all the real work around here. So why does that old Allis WC have her own stall in the machine shed? Oh, I have my reasons.

Excuse me...my nose is running and I'm a little choked up...allergies, you know. Be careful there...don't knock that shovel over against the Allis. Yeah, I know another dent in that battered sheet metal wouldn't even show. But...well, just be careful. That's Sweet Allis and she's something special, after all. She was my first.

Trying an International 706 Hi-Clear on for size at the state fair.

Cleveland Indians speedball pitcher and Baseball Hall of Famer Bob Feller sits at the controls of his Caterpillar Model Twenty. This tractor is similar to the one Feller grew up driving on his family's Iowa farm. *Ralph W. Sanders*

Caterpillar Hall of Fame

BY BOB FELLER

To baseball fans—and Caterpillar collectors—Bob Feller needs no introduction. Born and raised on a farm in Van Meter, Iowa, Feller stepped up to the pitching mound for the Cleveland Indians when he was a mere seventeen years old to throw what would quickly become a legendary fastball. After eighteen years with the Indians, Feller retired from baseball in 1956. Just six years later, he was elected to the Baseball Hall of Fame.

Feller has traveled the United States throwing baseballs, served in the U.S. Navy in the Pacific, and seen the bright lights of the big city. But you can't take the Iowa farm boy out of the man, and after his retirement from playing ball, Feller began to look back with a sense of nostalgia to the tractor he drove as a youth on his family's Iowa farm. That sentimentality inspired him to buy his first vintage Caterpillar, which led to purchasing a second one and eventually a whole fleet of old crawler iron.

When my father bought the first Caterpillar tractor in Iowa in the early 1930s to use on our family farm, everybody said he was crazy. "It won't work," folks told him. People in our part of the country drove Fordsons or Farmalls, Johnny Poppers or Olivers—tractors with wheels on them. Nobody used a Caterpillar with those crazy crawler treads on them. It simply wasn't right.

Well, naturally they were all wrong. That Cat Twenty proved itself on our farm and made a convert of me and many another farmer.

Our family's farm was located in the countryside near Van Meter in the south-central part of the state. Working our land, I put in many hours at the controls of that Cat Twenty, as well as the twelve-foot Caterpillar combine that my dad purchased to run with it. They were solid machines that served us well for many years. My fascination with Caterpillars grew from those roots and continues to grow today.

I left the family farm to earn my living throwing baseballs. When I was seventeen years old in 1936, I made my major league debut pitching for the Cleveland Indians against the St. Louis Cardinals. Over the years, I dueled from the pitching mound with some of the all-time greats, batters such as Ted Williams and Joe DiMaggio—just me against them. Some of the veterans of those days said I threw the fastest pitches they had ever seen.

We all took time out from baseball during the World War II years; I served with the U.S. Navy aboard the USS Alabama from December 1941 to August 1945. I returned to the mound in 1945 and remained true to the Cleveland Indians until my retirement from baseball in 1956. At the end of eighteen years of throwing fastballs for the Indians, I had a record of 266 wins against 162 losses, a lifetime ERA of 3.25, and 2,581 strikeouts. In 1962, I was elected to the Baseball Hall of Fame.

But despite my achievements on the baseball fields, part of my heart still belonged to the farm fields of my youth. Nostalgia for hallmarks of our roots seems to hit us harder as we grow older. For me, as for many farmers, one of the ties to my youth was the Caterpillar Twenty that I operated as a kid in the 1930s. I decided I wanted to track down another Twenty, which I soon did. Little did I know, but my life as a Cat collector had begun.

Since finding the Twenty, my small Caterpillar collection continues to grow. It's kind of my own personal Caterpillar "hall of fame" that includes my favorite Cat models: the Twenty, two Tens, a Forty, Twenty Two, Twenty Five, Twenty Eight, and a D4. Someday soon I hope to add to the collection.

You can look at the latest Caterpillar today and see the history in the machine. The lineage of the Holt and Best machines, the steam age, perfection of the crawler system, the early gas tractors, and Cat's industry-leading development of diesel power are all in a modern Cat. And that's part of what makes the Caterpillar story so great.

Another aspect of Caterpillar's greatest is that the machines are so versatile, a fact that is shown in the roster of Cat collectors. We come from all walks of life. Some come from a farming background. Other people's fascination with Cats started from working with them on construction sites, logging crews, road-grading jobs—anything and everything a Caterpillar can do.

The Moline
2-Wheel Tractor
Hitched to a
Moline 2-Bottom
Plow

Drivin' Tractor

BY MICHAEL PERRY

Humorist and writer Michael Perry is the author of the best-selling memoir *Population 485: Meeting Your Neighbors One Siren at a Time*, the essay collection *Off Main Street*, and the memoir *Truck: A Love Story*.

He has written for *Esquire*, The *New York Times Magazine*, *Outside*, and others, and is a contributing editor to *Men's Health*. His essays have been heard on National Public Radio's *All Things Considered*.

Raised on a small dairy farm, Perry equates his writing career to cleaning calf pens—just keep shoveling and eventually you've got a pile so big, someone will notice. He lives in rural Wisconsin, where he remains active as a volunteer firefighter and emergency medical responder.

Portions of this essay appeared in slightly modified form in *COOP: A Family, a Farm, and the Pursuit of One Good Egg* (HarperPerennial).

The equivalency is not absolute, but I'll pretty much guarantee you that for most farm kids the memory of the first time they "drove tractor" retains the approximate clarity of their first kiss. Me? Lisa Kettering, beneath a white pine in the moonlight on the road to Axehandle Lake, and: Jerry Coubal's John Deere B through the gate beside the Norway pine with the pigtail twist alongside the lane out back. Nicknamed Johnny Popper because of the distinctive two-cylinder *pop-pop-pop* of the exhaust, the tractor was a gangly looking machine with tall rear wheels and a slim front end supported by two wheels cambered to a narrow vee. The steering wheel was mounted in the near perpendicular and stood flat before your face like a clock on a wall. The square padded seat sat level with the top of the towering rear wheels, so you rode high, with a clear field of vision bisected only by the exhaust pipe, which pointed straight up in the air (between jobs we capped the pipe with a soup can—if the starter caught just right, the can would pop sky-high). Rather than a foot pedal, the B model had a hand clutch consisting of a slender steel rod capped with a round ball—rather like a solid iron walking stick. To engage the clutch you fed the walking stick forward; when you wanted to stop you pulled it backward, and the works disengaged with a steel-drum *ping!* Dad and his neighbor Jerry shared the Johnny Popper back and forth during haying season. One morning when I was nine years old I went out back to watch Dad rake the alfalfa. After he rolled the final windrow, he unhitched the rake and let me ride back with him. When we came to the gate beside the lane and the twisted Norway pine, Dad dismounted the tractor to open the gate as he always did, only this time after he swung it open he looked up at me and said, "Why don't you take 'er through?"

THE DEFINITION OF "FIRST" is subject to technicalities. Other tractors preceded the Johnny Popper. One hot summer day in 1967 my father snapped a shot of me sitting on Oliver Baalrud's John Deere Model AR—a squat machine with snug fenders and designed for orchard work. I was two years old, shod in green barn boots, sitting semi-sidesaddle, and pretending to steer. These were our first months on the farm. Dad—a city-raised boy—was green in every sense. When it came time to make hay, he says the neighbors just showed up. Oliver was driving the AR, which was attached to a gigantic New Holland baler equipped with its own pony engine and a voracious serrated plunger that rose and fell like a Tyrannosaurus Rex savaging a chicken.

In another scrapbook we have a black-and-white photo of the whole hay crew hooked in a line, five different tractors chained together trying to tug Oliver and the dinosaur baler from a low spot where his back wheels have spun into the muck. Everyone is cheerfully acknowledging the camera. Despite noble Depression-era paintings to the contrary, your rural agrarian-types come as flaw-riddled as any other average set of humans, but among the ones who raised me there was a lovely prevalent tendency to respond to any bad luck short of permanent injury with grins and delight. One time the steel pin securing the Tyrannosaurus head came loose, and the iron maw went angrily awry, slamming madly into the steel shroud as if the machine were intent on committing junkyard hari-kari. We took great delight in the mechanical carnage, and the alacrity with which Oliver leapt from his seat to kill the pony engine.

He didn't have to leap far. The AR's perforated steel seat protruded rearward to such an extent that when occupied by a large farmer the visual impression was that the machine was bound to pop a wheelie. Beneath the photograph pasted in my scrapbook, Mom wrote a caption explaining that I referred to the AR as "that *mig* John Deere *pup-pup* tractor."

The adjacent scrapbook photo is from a wider angle. In the foreground I can see a partial shadow of my father's head, identifiable by his protrusive left ear. The AR is in the background (now we can see it is hitched to the prehistoric New Holland) and I am sitting on a Murray chain-drive pedal tractor. In my memory the Murray is red—or maybe orange?—but the black-and-white photo is no help in that respect. It does have a single front wheel, so I can conclude that at some point my siblings and I wore it out, because I also recall a later Murray that was green, had dual front wheels, and was fitted with genuine fake spark plug wires. We drove the second one until the tin engine cowling broke loose from the frame and we had to hold the steering wheel up in order to keep the genuine fake spark plug wires from dragging in the dirt.

In the photo, the red-or-orange Murray tractor is hitched to a toy wagon and both are perfectly aligned with Oliver's baler and tractor in the background. I am a slightly pudgy toddler but staring off into the distance with a credible Eastwood squint. Inexplicably, I have stripped down to my underpants and am once again sitting sidesaddle. I cannot explain all the sidesaddling.

Funny, I start out writing about my one first tractor and now they're all coming back. At some point after we moved to the farm my brother and I found miniature International Farmall tractors beneath Grandma's Christmas tree. The steering wheels really worked, and the tires were rubber. Or rubber-like. There was even a hole in the hitch for a miniature pin. We ran them 'round and 'round, hooked to toy implements (a hay elevator with green plastic bales, a manure spreader with beaters that spun, a miniature baler irretrievably snarled with hair and lint) or carts of our own design. Every year by Christmas the Farmalls were pretty much shot, and every year Grandma—our city grandma—made sure replacements were under the tree. We were lucky kids.

MY FIRST MEMORY of a tractor is as solid as the day I formed it: I am running behind my father's Fordson as he plows the second field out past the town road that ran through our farm. I recall the feel of my feet in the furrow, the color of the soil shifting from red to tan as we moved from high ground to low, then the sound of the tractor lugging as the plow bit into the heavy black peat down around the pothole swamp. But locked in the slideshow of my mind is the angle of my father's torso as he braced his forearm against the fender. When I was conceived, Dad was in the Peace Corps. When I was born he was working in a paper mill. The day I captured him in that moment on that tractor, he became forevermore a farmer in my mind.

A YEAR LATER DAD took me out to mow hay. I balanced on his lap as he took the Fordson on its laps, the mower tight behind us on its three-point, the sickle chattering its vicious *snickety-snick*, the timothy stalks tumbling backward like some horizontal green waterfall. Dad let me rest my hands on the steering wheel but when we came to a corner I had to lift them clear while he spun the wheel hand-over-hand to the right and then back again as fast as he could in order to make the right-angle turn on the fly. One time I forgot to let go and Dad didn't notice. When he cranked into the turn, I hung on and was yanked from his lap and out into the space right in front of the back tire. Lightning-quick Dad snatched me from mid-air and dumped me back on his lap. I still retain the sense-memory of the tractor lurching to a stop and him cradling me belly-tight in one arm, the tractor motionless but roaring at full throttle. One irretrievable split-second thin-air swing into nothingness, and we were shaken as if in the wake of violence. Still tight in his arms, I looked up and saw in my father's face a mix of fear and abashment. My affection for tractors never dimmed, but from that moment I never mounted one without some subliminal part of me going on high alert. Later Dad would explain that Jerry—the farmer who took my father under his wing and became his best friend—lost his only son when the boy slipped from the fender to be crushed beneath the wheel.

It was possible to have a mishap on a tractor that ended in laughter. After I had been driving the John Deere B with its hand clutch for several years, Dad sent me out to cultivate corn with the neighbor's Allis-Chalmers WD-4. The Allis had a hand clutch as well, but it operated in the exact opposite direction: forward to stop, back to disengage. Anyone who has run machinery knows how quickly the body memorizes the motions of operation, so on the very first pass when I neared the end of the field I pulled on the hand clutch, intending to stop and count rows before making the turn. Nothing happened. I pulled again, harder. And then again. The tractor just kept motoring forward, and now the cultivator was tearing through the cross-rowed corn of the headlands. By now I was yanking at the hand clutch like a spastic robin trying to pull a six-foot worm. Things came to a safe resolution when the Allis dove nose-first into a drainage ditch, then rammed into the opposite bank and stalled out. I was still yanking the clutch. As tradition dictated, once it was determined that I was fine and the equipment damage was negligible, the incident was declared officially hilarious.

THE FIRST TRACTOR my father brought new was a gas-powered Massey-Ferguson 135. North Star Implement was still right in the heart of my hometown (New Auburn, Wisconsin, population then: 383) and it must have been sometime around 1976, because one of the tractors for sale was all spangled up in Bicentennial stars. Dad had been growing the farm for a while at this point and had a need to run some machinery the Fordson wasn't built to handle. In hindsight, the 135 was a relatively modest machine (designed to pull a three-bottom plow), but after the farm itself, it represented the single largest investment my father had ever made—especially in light of the fact that he was trying to raise a passel of kids on the income from eighteen cows and a small flock of sheep, *and* the fact that Dad refused to take out an equipment loan, preferring instead to scrape together the money one milk check at a time until he had enough. The advertisements in the farm magazines said the 135 was the world's bestselling tractor, "and you don't get there by being soft." Knowing my father as I do, I can assure you he bought the tractor in *spite* of such rhetoric.

The 135 had a square, sturdy look. The ads referred to the "control center" but this description was a tad grand: what you had was a steering wheel and a throttle stick, a knob for the lights, and a handful of illuminated dials. The cowling and fenders were painted a rich red, and dead-center on the black-and-silver striped grille was the triple-triangle logo featuring a tractor with a raised plow to commemorate the three-point hitch system developed by Harry Ferguson. Of all the tractors in my childhood, I put in more hours on the Massey than any other. A few years after Dad purchased it, I came into an age where I could be relied on to operate unsupervised afield. I covered our little farm again and again, pulling a disc or a drag, laying down swathes of tall grass with the haybine, or making the daily run out back with the manure spreader. Few memories of the farm are fonder than those of the nights I would pull the drag over freshly tilled fields deep into the night, my whole world contained in the pool of light shed by the Massey's front and rear lights, the heat from the crankcase warming me even as cold fog seeped through the bottomlands (some summer days the Massey ran so hot you could see the gasoline boiling in the glass sediment filter). How adult I felt when I'd pull into the yard well after dark knowing that I had helped my overworked father pull ahead or at least keep even with the spring planting.

And it was upon the tractor above all places that I had time to sort my tumultuous teenage heart. Years later, when I was as far from the farm life as I've ever been, I wrote a quite awful poem that nonetheless still brings a smile to my face. A mercifully short portion: . . . *that tractor would be a plunging white charger in plowing daydreams where you waited to be rescued at the end of every row . . .*

I doubt I was the only young man who filled my hours on the tractor with thoughts beyond agriculture. This will explain the occasional zigzag furrow. . . .

I AM REMEMBERING MY father at the kitchen table. I am still relatively small because I can also recall looking up past the shiny silver edge of the kitchen table and into the fluorescent light above his head. He was plowing, he is telling my mother, and the oil plug worked itself loose. He heard a knocking from the engine, looked in panic at the oil pressure gauge, saw the needle sunk to nothing, switched the tractor off in an instant. I heard him say it might be "froze up." That he couldn't judge the damage until the mechanics at the dealership pulled the headers. I don't really understand the conversation, but I am rooted in place because Dad's voice is taut in a way I have not heard before.

In the end, he didn't take the tractor in. He got another plug, changed the oil filter, put in fresh oil, and then—heart beating, he admits—tried the starter. The engine took, and he ran it briefly, then changed the filter, repeated the process, changed the filter again, and ran the engine again. First time around, the filter yielded up a few flakes of iron, then nothing, and no trouble in the decades that followed. "I did everything with that tractor," he said, when he finally sold it. For all my fond memories of the 135, the most *meaningful* is that of the night he lost the oil plug. Thinking of him at that table, the house full of kids and not a penny to spare, all the money sunk in that tractor. That tractor was the *farm*. And the farm was the family. I could hear all of that in Dad's voice. It made my insides feel as pale and tremulous as the light from those fluorescents. And yet the power of the memory today isn't that I sensed my father was scared, it is that I sensed he was *human*—and thus I cherish it.

TIME CAME WHEN the farms dwindled. Fewer and fewer farmers walked into North Star Implement looking to buy a tractor. Toward the end, most of the tractors on the lot were decades old—vintage models kept in stock in hopes that they might catch the eye of weekenders headed for their little patch of land "up north." Maybe get themselves a vintage Fordson for scraping the driveway, or a row-crop Allis that matched the gazebo. Eventually, even those sales weren't enough, and the dealership closed up for good.

It is a perpetual matter of humanity, the cycling interplay of regret and reminiscence. The same old feelings, applied in altered circumstances. My Grandpa Peterson spent the bulk of his career driving a government-issue desk. But when we gathered around the recliner in his retirement

years, his recollections invariably wound back to his boyhood days in the
field driving Fanny and Daisy and Ol' Bill. Seven decades removed, and
he was still animated by the memory of how those horses handled, and
what power he felt when he took the leather straps in his hands. He never
drove a tractor in his youth, but his memories are just the same as mine
regarding the Johnny Popper. And just as Grandpa would have said no
tractor could compete with the flesh and blood of those broad-backed
horses, I am tempted to say that today's computerized behemoths can't
hold a candle to a coughing two-cylinder . . . but somewhere the affections survive even as the *object* of those affections change. You figure
somewhere some prehistoric old-timer spent time reminiscing about his
finest digging stick. I reckon we don't miss the stick so much as the digging. Either way, we are following a continuous thread traced in the dirt.

"WHY DON'T YOU TAKE 'ER through?"

I still remember the offhand way my father uttered the words, and
how the adrenaline surged through me when I heard them. I realize now
that he was probably anticipating my wide eyes.

The John Deere B was a good starter tractor, because you didn't have
to reach any pedals. The tall hand clutch, the position of the steering
wheel, and a broad steel deck between the seat and the steering column
made it possible to operate from a standing position—in fact when I
was older I often drove standing up if only because I could fantasize that
rather than some hayfield in Sampson Township one was navigating the
Mississippi in a Mark Twain paddlewheeler.

Back there at that gate, with the John Deere going *pop . . . pop . . .
pop* at low idle, I addressed the wheel with knees trembling. Reaching
down to the gear selector, I ran it through its cast-iron maze and into
first. Then, with one hand on the steering wheel and heart tripping, I
pushed that hand clutch slowly, slowly ahead until sure enough the green
machine was inching forward, and there I was, *driving tractor*. The gate
was plenty wide but I felt like I was piloting the Queen Mary through a
checkout lane at the IGA. When I made safe passage—head swiveling
left, right, left to make sure I hadn't snapped the fenceposts—I *pinged* the
clutch out of gear with a combination of exhilaration and relief. Dad took
the wheel back for the ride home and I rode happily on his lap, still his
small boy but much taller in my heart.

Family Portraits

The family aboard the Fordson.

The whole family goes tractor shopping at the state fair, a Styled Deere Model B catching their eye.

The family poses with its newest member, a Ford Model NAA.

The family proudly poses with the Joliet tractor.

The kids climb aboard the family Massey-Harris 44 for a picture.

Memories of a
Former Kid

BY BOB ARTLEY

For several decades now, artist Bob Artley has collected his reminiscences of the farming life into a syndicated cartoon series entitled "Memories of a Former Kid" that originated from the *Worthington Daily Globe* newspaper in Worthington, Minnesota. His drawings and essays have also been collected into several books, including *Memories of a Former Kid* and *A Book of Chores As Remembered by a Former Kid*.

These cartoons recall the day when the tractor—in this case, a Fordson—came to stay on the Artley farm and soon became part of the family.

Tractor Lessons

BY MARGRET ALDRICH

Margret Aldrich is an editor and writer living in Minneapolis, Minnesota, with her husband, Gary, and sons Abe, age three, and Asher, age one. While Margret enjoys driving her VW station wagon, she looks back fondly on the days of driving tractor on the family farm near Beaver, Iowa. In this story, history repeats itself as her dad gives Margret and then Abe their very first tractor lessons. Driver's ed was never so much fun. . . .

"The first thing you need to learn about driving a tractor is how to shut it off," my dad said matter-of-factly, looking me straight in the eye and pointing a finger at my nose. This was how he began my inaugural tractor-driving lesson, which was a rite of passage for every farmkid. I knew that this was serious business.

It was summertime in central Iowa, and I had just finished fourth grade. The corn, soybeans, and alfalfa were in the ground; our flock of sheep was in the pasture; and since Dad had some extra time on his hands (and a ten-year-old girl to entertain), he thought this might be a good time to begin tractor-driving lessons. I had been on a tractor plenty—sitting on Dad's lap and "helping" him steer as he plowed a field or drove a wagon of beans the two miles to the elevator—but I hadn't been tall enough to reach the clutch and brake pedals and, therefore, hadn't been old enough for driving lessons. Like the amusement park signs that said, "You must be this high to ride," I had to pass the clutch-pedal test before I would be allowed to pilot the tractor.

So, before he imparted any further tractor wisdom, he motioned for me to climb up into the driver's seat of the IH Farmall 806D and show him that I could press the clutch all the way to the floor. I pulled myself up into the seat. It felt good up there. I looked to my right at our farmhouse and felt about as tall as the third-floor attic window. Over my left shoulder, I saw our border collie patrolling around the sheep in the east pasture, subtly herding them into a loose group. I enjoyed the scene for just a moment then took a deep breath, grabbed onto the steering wheel, and stomped on the clutch as hard as I could. It groaned as I pushed it down, down, down—all the way to the floor.

"All right," said Dad, "that means you're ready!" In one motion, he climbed up beside me and started up the engine, because, as he had promised, our first lesson would be shutting it off.

"How do you think you do it?" he said over the roar of the engine.

"Turn the key off!" I yelled. I tried, but the key didn't do it.

Dad moved the long throttle handle behind the steering wheel all the way to the left to cut off the fuel supply, and the engine stopped. He started it up again and let me kill the engine. Lesson one, check! I was anxious to get moving and tear out of the gravel driveway.

Well, as with most tractors, that Farmall wasn't exactly going to tear anywhere. I suppose that was the beauty of teaching me to drive a tractor rather than one of my grandpa's beat-up drag-racing cars. I wouldn't be moving fast enough to do any damage. The rest of the lesson creeped along, too, and went something like this.

Step one: Turn on the key so the battery connects to the starter.

Step two: Move the throttle a little to the right so the engine gets some fuel.

Step three: Push the clutch pedal all the way down until it engages the safety switch.

Step four: Keep your right hand on the steering wheel for bracing. Then with your free hand, push in the starter button.

With my skinny fourth-grade leg standing on the clutch, I had the best of intentions, but you know how the next few minutes went: Start, chug, stall. Start, chug, stall. Start, chug, stall. Until, finally, the tractor lurched forward, hiccupped, and kept going, breathing a black, smokey sigh of relief from its stack. We were on the move! Dad helped me steer the tractor onto the main road and then let me bump the throttle up bit by bit. The tractor roared louder and louder, vibrating every tooth in my head and every bone in my body. There was no sign of stalling now—I glanced down at the big back tires, and they seemed to be spinning at breakneck speed. On either side of the road, black fields were lined with straight, healthy rows of new plants, and red-winged blackbirds watched us from the fence posts.

We drove like that for a while, Dad offering up comments about the soybean crop or the cows eating grass near Beaver Creek, me loosening my white-knuckle grip on the steering wheel ever so slightly.

Then, trouble. (I might have gasped, but the tractor was too loud for anyone to hear it.) Coming toward us was a big green machine—our neighbor, Mr. Hunter, on his new John Deere. My heart raced as I wondered how two tractors could possibly pass each other on that thin strip of gravel. We chugged closer. And closer. I felt like I was playing the slowest game of chicken the world had ever seen. I could read the seed logo stitched onto Mr. Hunter's cap. I could see the dirt of a morning's work on his face. Dad guided the tractor farther and farther to the right, until I was sure we were going to topple over into the ditch. Our Farmall and Mr. Hunter's Deere finally met, with merely inches (I was sure of it) separating them. And then, the most wonderful thing happened: As our tractors squeaked by each other, Mr. Hunter looked at me, offered the hint of a smile, and lifted his index finger off of the steering wheel to say hello. I finger-waved back. The rite of passage was complete; I was a real farmkid now.

As the years went by, I graduated to faster-moving vehicles. By age twelve, I was allowed to drive Dad's 1960 Chevy pick-up by myself as long as I stuck to gravel roads. If I had a friend with me, we were allowed to drive it only in the pasture. That was safe for innocent bystanders, but not for that poor old pickup. My best friend and I drove it as fast as we could over every bump in the field, knocking our heads on the ceiling and knocking the battery on top of the engine. It was a long walk to the house to tell my dad about that one; it made me think I should have stuck with tractors.

These days, I live in Minneapolis with my husband, Gary, and two young sons, but my parents are still on the farm. Not much has changed there, happily enough. The Farmall 806D and the '60 Chevy are still around, though they're now housed in a Morton building instead of the gray, weathered barn. The red-winged black-birds still watch the comings and goings on the stretch of gravel that runs past the farmhouse, though the road is now called 210th Street instead of Rural Route 1. My husband, boys, and I like to visit as often as we can, and we celebrate every Christmas there. I particularly love being at the farmhouse toward the end of the summer, when the corn is high in the south field and the fireflies are thick in the evenings.

This summer, my oldest son Abe was two and a half when we were on the farm. Old enough to walk out to the old sheep barn with the dog (and me not too far behind); old enough to eat three ears of corn on the cob in one sitting; and old enough, I found out, to learn how to drive tractor.

Although he wasn't even close to passing the clutch-pedal test, my dad (ever after known as Grandad) thought it was about time Abe had his first tractor lesson.

"That's all right with me," I said, and the two headed off to the machine shed.

"Now, Abe," I heard my dad say. "When we're done, I want you to tell me if the tractor was loud or if it was quiet."

"Okay, Grandad," Abe answered, as he practically galloped to the big, red tractor.

Abe scaled the Farmall and looked, I thought, particularly small in the driver's seat with my dad. The two had a grand time. Abe took his steering duties quite seriously, only taking a hand off the wheel to wave at Gary and me as they left the driveway and headed for open road, his smile stretching from ear to ear.

When they finally pulled back into the driveway and turned off the tractor, my dad posed the question, "So, Abe, was the tractor loud or was it quiet?"

"It was LOUD, Grandad!" Abe answered approvingly.

Later that night, Gary jokingly asked my dad why he had never been invited to drive the Farmall. Apparently, Gary had never driven a tractor before.

"What?" Dad exclaimed. "Never driven a tractor? Well, don't you worry, Gary. I'll be sure you get to drive the Farmall all you want at Christmastime. And I'll be sure there's a snow blade on it."

When we got back to Minneapolis after that visit, Abe was already thinking about the next time he would get to drive tractor with Grandad. I wondered if we should start practicing the index-finger wave, just to be prepared.

We put some pictures of Abe and the Farmall in a photo album and, later, I overheard him showing them to a friend.

"That's me, that's Grandad, and that's MY tractor," he explained. Could this former farmgirl's heart be any more filled with pride?

Grandpa Aldrich teaches young Abe to drive the family Farmall 806D. *Gary J. Kunkel*

Advertisement for Ertl's Elvis Presley Deere 4010 toy tractor.

Elvis's Tractor

BY JOHN DIETZ

Elvis Presley should need no introduction. And if you're that one in a million person who does need an introduction to Elvis, where have you been living—under a haybale? But Elvis's tractor probably does need some explaining.

Most everyone knows that Elvis hailed from Mississippi, and while he was not a farm boy exactly, coming from farm country left its mark on him. Everyone's heard tales of Elvis's many motorcycles and cars—Harley-Davidsons, Cadillacs of every color, Lincoln Continentals, even a De Tomaso Pantera he once shot with a pistol when it wouldn't start. But here, for the first time, is the story of Elvis's John Deere.

"Elvis Presley had a tractor?" A few responses were like that as I searched for the scoop on Elvis and his tractors. The whole subject came to attention in early 2009 when a shining green-and-yellow 1963 John Deere 4010 tractor was unveiled at Graceland. The restoration had been a joint project of Elvis Presley Enterprises, Inc. (EPE) and Deere & Company. An unlikely pairing, two of the biggest names in hardcore entertainment and hardcore machinery, but there it was.

Everybody knew Elvis was a poor country boy from the South. They knew about Graceland, the mega-tourist attraction that's like one of the Seven Wonders of the Modern World; in a lifetime if you're lucky, you can walk around the base of the Great Pyramid or the floor of the Parthenon, or take a boat below Niagara Falls, or do an escorted tour of Graceland.

Behind the scenes, Graceland had an old dusty and rusty faded green tractor doing a bit of yard work. If a visitor noticed it, the tractor probably seemed out of place in the manicured, candied-up 13.8-acre extravaganza of mansion, trees, and lawn in south Memphis. Graceland hasn't moved in the past 60 years, but most things around it have. It has been incorporated into the Memphis metropolis, hedged in by comfortable new homes and suburban sprawl. Old State Highway 51 north-south still goes past the front door, though it's now known as Elvis Presley Boulevard. Two miles east of Graceland, the little Memphis Airport has morphed into Memphis International Airport. Downtown is still 5 miles north, and the Mississippi state line still is only 3 miles south, and the Mississippi River still snakes slowly along about 8 miles east of Graceland.

That dusty old tractor, however, did have a story and still does. That particular John Deere 4010 is a row crop diesel that was built at the John Deere Waterloo Tractor Works, in Waterloo, Iowa, and shipped to the Planters Tractor John Deere dealership in Tunica, Mississippi, on March 12, 1963. Tunica is in the heart of the Delta Blues country, about 2 miles east of the Muddy Mississippi and on the fringe of a growing casino/resort area. The little town, population around 1,200, is about 45 miles southwest of Graceland. The dealership changed hands in 1985 and continues today as Parker Tractor.

The approximate base price for the 1963 John Deere 4010 tractor was $5,711. This included the tractor with syncro-range transmission, wide front end adjustable front axle, three-point hitch, two remote cylinders with hoses, deluxe fenders, lamps, and deluxe seat. It was the largest and most popular of four models in John Deere's "New Generation of Power" tractors. These were four- and six-cylinder tractors that the company introduced in 1960 and that helped propel the company to become the world's leading manufacturer of farming equipment. They replaced the venerable two-cylinder tractors that had established a solid reputation and market share for the Midwestern manufacturer since 1924.

The Elvis Presley tractor is one of 57,573 units of the 4010 that were built in a three-year run (1961–1963). There were variations during the production run, with choices for three types of fuel (gas, diesel, or propane) and three body configurations for American farms (row crop, standard, or Hi-Crop). The tractor acquired by Elvis is listed by the internal production code as a Series 213, meaning it was configured as a row-crop tractor with a diesel-fueled engine. Factory records indicate that Deere built 36,736 units in Series 213 tractors. The diesel engine produced 84 horsepower.

The tractor was equipped with a 46A John Deere loader. The 46A was a light duty, single-cylinder loader unit, with bucket, for New Generation 10 Series tractors. Over the years, few of the loaders have survived. This may be a unique model, in that the loader survived with the bucket and a manure scoop attached to the front of the bucket. The original manure scoop was equipped with seven tines. In the 1960s, the approximate cost for the loader was $537. The serial number provided by Graceland indicates the loader was purchased later than the tractor.

The Elvis tractor at Graceland was first purchased new by Jack A. Adams. The 4010 was included in the deal when Adams sold his little ranch to Elvis Presley in 1967.

GRACELAND TRACTOR

By the time Elvis discovered Adams' For Sale sign at Twinkletown Farms, he had been a star of stage, screen, and television for more than 10 years. His rock 'n' roll, a mixture of high energy southern gospel, blues, and Dixie, catapulted the dirt-poor young Elvis from East Tupelo, Mississippi, into fame and early wealth. Even I remember Elvis hitting like a lightning bolt on the Ed Sullivan show in late 1956, at age 21. Memphis, about a hundred miles northwest of Tupelo, was his recording headquarters. Elvis turned to his parents, Vernon and Gladys Presley, to find an appropriate home. In March 1957, he purchased a stately old Memphis mansion at their recommendation for $102,000. His cousin Patsy Presley Geranen recalled that Elvis "always associated Graceland with his mother, my aunt Gladys. Remember, we were Depression poor people from Tupelo. When Elvis's records got popular, among the first things he did was buy Aunt Gladys a pink Cadillac, pretty dresses, and nice jewelry. He wanted to buy her the world."

Elvis also was a hands-on-the-wheel country boy. He'd drive just about anything with an engine and ride the rest. He drove everything from dune buggies to tractors to bulldozers. Owning serious property for the first time in his life, and full of energy, Elvis took on some outside renovations to the property at Graceland himself before moving in.

Apparently, his first tractor at Graceland was an International. In a 1957 home movie, Elvis is seen riding on what appears to be a new, bright red, mid-size International Harvester model 300 tractor. The IH 300 utility tractor production years were 1954 to 1956. The four-cylinder engine had 30 horsepower on the drawbar and could handle a three-bottom plow or, in this case, a wide three-point hitch-mounted rototiller.

Bruce Marren posted the film on YouTube in August 2007. According to Marren, the original was shot on 8mm film by a "Davidson" family while driving from St Louis to Florida. They found Elvis working with his tractor on a warm day, filmed, and saved the footage.

It begins with five seconds of Elvis driving the tractor along a wooded hillside, without a shirt, apparently at Graceland. A power-takeoff operated rototiller, intended for use with large gardens, is attached to the tractor's three-point hitch. Elvis drives the tractor around a large tree, turning, and heads down the gently sloping hillside out of sight. In the main segment that follows, about 30 seconds, the tractor is stuck in a short mud hole and Elvis is seen working at releasing it from the mud. Eventually, he backs it out and then drives forward past the camera operator. In the final 30 seconds, Col. Tom Parker, driving a big white Cadillac, stops at the gates of Graceland to greet the family.

"The original footage was very fast and jerky, so I slowed it down by 50 percent," said Marren in personal correspondence. He added, "The family did talk with Elvis. I was told the father suggested a few ways to get his tractor out of the mud."

The early Graceland tractor is mentioned, but not identified, by authors Peter Guralnick and Ernst Jorgensen, in *Elvis Day by Day: The Definitive Record of His Life and Music*. They wrote that on Monday, April 15, 1957 (p. 104): "Elvis visits his new estate, posing for photographs with a fan while sitting on a tractor he has just purchased for work around the grounds."

Depending on how you read it, up to three more tractors appear in the Elvis story in early 1967, prior to the time he acquired the John Deere 4010. In January 1967, *Elvis Day by Day* records that Elvis had the area behind Graceland cleared and bulldozed for a new riding arena, while work was continuing on a barn. It's unclear whether the 'bulldozed' refers to a tractor or a dozer, whether Elvis owned it, and whether he operated it. However, on Saturday, February 4, the authors state: "In order to enlarge the riding arena behind Graceland, several small buildings, including the house where Billy Smith once lived, are bulldozed, with Elvis gleefully taking part in the work." Then, on Monday after the weekend, *Elvis Day By Day* states that "Elvis buys a white buckskin horse and a quarter horse named Conchita's Gold, as well as a Case tractor and two El Camino pickup trucks."

Tractors also are mentioned in the recollections of three members of the Elvis entourage. The tractors are not identified.

Elvis and the Memphis Mafia, an oral history compiled by author Alanna Nash, contains memories of first cousin Billy Smith, Memphis Mafia foreman Marty Lacker and Lamar Fike, who joined the army with Elvis. They accompanied Elvis nearly every day from 1956 to his death in 1977. Twice, they mentioned Elvis and a tractor.

Lamar Fike, recalling the first months at Graceland: "Elvis was always pushing the limit. I don't think he was trying to be macho. I think it was letting off steam. When he moved into Graceland, he got out there on a big tractor with a bush-hog on it and cleaned the back acreage. Then he decided he'd tear down the old back fence. He hooked a chain around the fence posts and then to the tractor and pulled them out of the ground.

"Finally, he hooked the chain around the corner post and began to pull. He didn't realize it was set in concrete. The tractor bucked and almost turned over on him. He was just teetering there for a second. You knew when something scared the crap out of him because he'd start laughing. Gladys ran out, screaming, 'Elvis, get off that damn tractor and put it up right now!' He was white as goose down. He climbed off and put his arms around Gladys and said, 'I'm OK, Satnin.' I'm OK.' He never thought anything would happen to him.'"

Another recalled, at the Circle G ranch: "There were some people having a party, so he just pulled the tractor up to their window and we serenaded the whole bunch. Then Elvis tipped his hat and we drove off."

Marty Lacker said, "Elvis had a couple of months before he had to go do his next picture, which was *Clambake*, and he spent almost every day down at the ranch. It was winter. We had a little office by the stable, and I remember, at two o'clock in the morning, we were standing outside there. It was snowing, and Elvis was on a small tractor, pushing the snow and mud out of the way. Some of us were just standing there, watching him do this. And Vernon walked out of the office and came up to me with an adding machine tape in one hand and a flashlight in the other. He was, like, whining. He said, 'Marty, look at this! He's spent $98,000 on trucks and given them away.' I said, 'What do you want me to do? He's your son.'"

FLYING CIRCLE G

Elvis was inducted into the U.S. Army in March 1958, less than a year after moving into Graceland. After his discharge in March 1960, he was traveling almost constantly. Front pages of newspapers and magazines were filled with President Kennedy, the Civil Rights Movement, the start of a war in South Vietnam; inside, Elvis "The King" Presley led the entertainment news.

When he could be home in Graceland, along with a few close friends, he enjoyed the outdoors and outdoor life. He treated his friends well, making sure they had a good time at Graceland. Super-charged golf carts became bumper cars and racing machines on the Graceland turf. Go-carts roared around the circular Graceland driveway. Then Elvis bought a horse, and a second, and he discovered a new fascination. Call it the Cowboy Life.

Friend and author Jerry Schilling wrote in *Me And A Guy Named Elvis*:

"As more horses joined the Graceland herd, more work needed to be done on the barn and on the fences. And when I think about favorite times with Elvis, this period always jumps to mind. Here was Elvis Presley, finding satisfaction in wiping cobwebs out of an old barn, in nailing up planks and painting fence posts. We'd spend hours together in the afternoon, just going through all the basic chores of horse care: checking their water, forking over their hay, brushing out their coats...

"Sometimes, walking through the Graceland kitchen, I'd find a yellow legal pad on the counter with personal notes from Elvis making me aware of what job needed to be handled next: 'We need to get three bridles,' 'We need more horse blankets,' 'We need stirrups to match the bridles' would be written out in red. Elvis wasn't a guy who usually left notes for anybody—but the last thing he'd do each night was write these out, so that every detail he thought of would get taken care of.

"After working all day, we'd often go back out to the freezing cold of the barn bundled up in our jackets and cowboy hats. We'd sit around a little bucket of fire out there, with our feet up, passing the time away. Sometimes Priscilla and Sandy—whose gift horses had started all this— were down there with us. One of them would make coffee and we'd huddle together and sip from our mugs. Sometimes a few of the guys would hang out together down there, having a laugh. And sometimes it was just Elvis and me next to the fire, talking away like we had on that very first cross-country trip. Sure, I loved the limos, and the mansions, and the movie life, and the VIP treatment everywhere we went. But this simple cowboy life was just as satisfying, and everything I loved about our friendship was right there in that freezing, freshly painted barn.

"I felt Elvis had created something great with the barn and the horses—he'd given himself a perfect way to escape the pressures and burdens that built up on him outside of those stables. But it was just impossible for him to say, 'This is just right.' Instead, he must have felt that if having ten horses was a good thing, having twenty would be even better, and having thirty would be even better than that. We kept going out and buying more animals and more gear, and our trips started happening during typical Elvis hours—we'd often be down in Mississippi somewhere riding potential purchases at three in the morning.

"On one of those trips, Elvis and Priscilla, Sandy and I, and Alan Fortas went out, driving down to the renowned Lennox Farms in Mississippi to find a Tennessee Walker for Vernon. It was just about daybreak as we headed back toward Graceland piled together in that big old double-cab pickup truck. Alan was driving, and all of a sudden Elvis told him to pull off the road. When Alan did so, Elvis pointed out the passenger window. Right away we all saw what he saw—a huge white cross towering over some rolling green hills as pristine as a golf course. The first rays of sunlight were glinting off a rippling lake in the center of the property, and there was one perfectly quaint little farmhouse close to the road. There was also a FOR SALE sign up. Elvis got that look in his eye—the one that meant he'd just put a plan together.

" 'Alan,' he said. 'Go knock on the door of that house. Tell them you want to buy this place. But don't tell them it's for me.' "

Elvis had discovered Twinkletown Farms. The date was February 9, 1967. Within days, the farm, the John Deere 4010 tractor, and a herd of Santa Gertrudis cattle belonged to Elvis. He named it Circle G Ranch, and adjusted that to Flying Circle G due to a name registration conflict. [There were at least three 'G's in his life: Gladys, Graceland, and God.] Within weeks, the Circle G was home to 40 horses, along with trucks, tractors, trailers, and fresh-from-the-store ranch gear.

The Circle G site today is mostly hidden in the open, along the east side of Highway 301 and south of West Goodman Road (Hwy 302). It's just two miles south of the Mississippi border with Tennessee, and 10 miles south of Graceland. The square, half-mile, mostly undeveloped quarter-section has open pastures, clusters of tall hardwood trees, and a large irregular pond covering about 10 to 14 acres.

At age 90, in 2009, Jack Adams still recalled the ranch at Horn Lake and his encounters with Elvis.

Adams said the place had been "prettied up" as his get-away in the years before Elvis saw it. Adams called it Twinkletown Farms. It was about half-way between home and his office at the Twinkletown Airport in Walls, Mississippi. Adams acquired the farm while working as a commercial pilot for Chicago & Southern Airlines (Delta Airlines today). He resigned from Delta Airlines in 1963. Adams was operating a successful used airplane business from the airport, when he and Elvis struck a deal on the property.

"It was a beautiful piece of property," Adams said. "There was a little country home that I had remodeled and redone. It had a pretty good lake (that I had built) and a bridge across the lake and a great big cross that sat right on the south side of the lake. It had 150 head of Santa Gertrudis cattle, too. We had a lot of people there, and a lot of fun. That little lake was fresh and clean; I had a 10-inch well that pumped water into it, and I had it stocked with trout. It was a beautiful place."

A chain link fence supported by white concrete pillars surrounded the entire property. The irregular 10-acre lake that Elvis saw was behind a small dam that Adams had constructed. A white, low-level steel-and-concrete footbridge, about 300 feet long, crossed the narrower part of the lake. About a hundred feet from the end of the lake, beyond the footbridge, Elvis could see a white concrete cross. It was about 75 feet tall. Both the bridge and the cross were lighted by at night, Adams said.

The cross served as a place for Adams' personal devotions. It's a little "rugged" today but still standing on a knoll near the lake and framed by trees. "God told me to build it," Adams said. "It was well constructed. It was really pretty to see. I had a gentleman build it in Memphis. They hauled it down here and set it up so it was free-standing."

The package of 160-acre ranch, fence, pond, bridge, cross, cattle, cottage, and equipment came with an eye-popping price ($437,000) but it gave Elvis the space for his new passion, horses, and the place for his honeymoon with Priscilla, surrounded by his entourage of musicians, managers, and assistants. For a couple weeks, Elvis considered building a modern home on his Mississippi ranch and giving an acre to each friend in his entourage so they could build homes, too, and live in a kind of communal setting.

Elvis soon had eight trailers sitting at the south end of the property on concrete pads, hooked to gas and electricity and close to the lake shore. Cousin Billy Smith and family moved into the cottage at the north end, close to the highway. Elvis and Priscilla, instead, moved into a double-wide, three-bedroom trailer complete with white picket fence for their honeymoon in May.

For Adams, there's more than a land transaction to remember. Details about the property—and the tractor that went with it—have faded but he remembers the young couple who bought it.

"Elvis was a very, very fine, humble, pleasant, clean cut young man," Adams said. "He did exactly what he said he would do. He was really a nice gentleman. And the people that were with him were real nice.

"I took he and his wife riding in a little Hughes helicopter that I had. They loved it, too. For about three Sundays consecutively, they had me flying it. Priscilla was petite, just a darling little human being. We just enjoyed one another."

Schilling said, "Elvis loved to take on a challenging project, he loved to spend money, and he loved to have the people he loved around him. The ranch gave him a chance to have all of that at once, and as things settled down a bit, there were some good times. Elvis was active and having fun, and Priscilla, Sandy, and I, along with Alan, Marty, Red, Larry Geller, Mike Keaton, Richard Davis, Joe and Joanie Esposito, and Billy and Jo Smith got into the spirit, too, spending a lot of time on horseback. The horses were trained and looked after by Mike McGregor, a professional horseman and saddler who became a well-liked and much-appreciated member of the group—the Circle G's answer to the Marlboro Man. There were picnics, barbecues, target shooting, snake hunts—a lot of nice, easygoing, outdoorsy moments."

Authors Laura Levin and John O'Hara wrote in *Elvis and You: Your Guide to the Pleasures of Being an Elvis Fan*:

"For him, it (the Circle G) was a perfect retreat from Hollywood and he was thrilled to move back to Mississippi. The peacefulness and back-to-nature activities soothed him. Elvis enjoyed his time at the ranch riding horses in God's country, as he called it. He enjoyed it so much, he didn't want to leave; he spent many happy days playing cowboy with his friends. Elvis and Priscilla spent part of their honeymoon there, preferring to stay in one of the mobile homes instead of the main house. It is speculated that Lisa Marie may have been conceived in that mobile home. Privacy again became an issue and Elvis was forced to build a 10-foot-high wooden fence around the property to keep the fans at bay. He ended up selling the ranch two years after the purchase when he grew tired of it and it had become too much of a financial burden."

The idyll, in fact, ended in only a few months. The property was soon besieged by fans and salesmen. According to *The Elvis Encyclopedia*, "Elvis spent early 1967 buying more than three dozen pick-up trucks for himself, his relatives, his entourage and farm workers for use on the newly-acquired Circle G ranch. …When the guys got bored of racing their horses, they'd drag race their pick-up trucks, or attempt stunts on the tractor. Things really began to unravel when entourage members and their wives began wanting to get back to their normal lives. By the summer, Elvis had returned to his usual Memphis pursuits of watching movies and hanging out with his pals at Graceland, and the ranch was put up for sale."

Markers of Elvis's short idyll at the Circle G still can be seen. Somewhere on the property, a red brick barbecue bears the initials EP. And, from the highway, a gleaming white footbridge can be seen crossing just above the pond. A sign at the bridge tells this story: "Bridge erected as a short cut across the lake. Elvis crossed it once riding 'Sun' while it was covered with snow & ice. It was always lighted." Out of direct sight now from the highway, the tall old weathered cross still was standing in early 2010. The shadow of the cross can be seen in aerial views on the Google Maps search engine.

Equipment and farm paraphernalia was auctioned off on November 4, 1967, raising $108,000. By Christmas 1967, the ranch was shut down and out of Elvis's life—less than a year after its purchase. The remaining horses were moved back to Graceland, where Elvis and everyone else continued to ride in the fields behind the mansion. A sale in 1969 fell through but the property was finally sold by the Presleys in 1973 to the Boyle Investment Company.

Recalling that November 1969 auction in 2009, a tractor enthusiast wrote in the *Yesterday's Tractors* forum: "I was going to NCR school in Memphis in 1967. There was a large machinery sale on Elvis's ranch one Sat., so I went. There were two 4010s and a 4020 that sold."

TRACTOR RIDES

After the Circle G days, Graceland again was home for Elvis. The John Deere 4010 that he acquired with the Circle G came to Graceland when Elvis sold the ranch. He used it frequently, and it continued to be in daily service as a tractor at Graceland until late 2008.

"That 4010 has had a great lifespan," said Kevin Kern, director of public relations at Elvis Presley Enterprises. "We've always considered it an artifact, but it also was a great piece of equipment. It was a workhorse and did a great job, but the time came to have it fully restored up at Northwest Mississippi Community College, where John Deere has a program.

"Elvis loved to be on the property here at Graceland. He had 13.8 acres on which Graceland sits, and he used it all. There were horses, there was the tractor, and there were golf carts. Elvis liked to be on anything that moved, and that included the John Deere tractor.

"It's said that Elvis took the tractor and bulldozed an empty house down with the front end loader. When he got on a whim and decided it was time for that place to come down, he made it happen. He didn't wait for anybody else to do it. That was Elvis Presley.

"But, Elvis probably spent more time taking people for rides than he would have doing any work with the tractor. He was well known for taking people on rides on the tractor. It was a favorite pastime for him, then, even though it wouldn't be approved today for safety reasons. He loved to entertain people on stage, as we all know, but when he had visitors at Graceland he wanted them to have fun here as well. He had riding horses, the golf carts, or the John Deere tractor.

"There are many stories told about Elvis using the tractor and having great fun. For instance—this isn't safe, and the equipment is not intended for this purpose—he'd have people sit in the front loader, and a child might ride on a lap. It's not exactly the safest, but they'd move slowly. We don't have any pictures of that, but Elvis loved taking charge and using the tractor."

Jimmy Gambill, maintenance director at Graceland and second cousin to Elvis, worked directly with the 4010 for most of three decades. After the restoration was completed, he shared some of his own boyhood memories of Elvis and the tractor with the restoration team.

"Elvis loved that tractor," Gambill told the team. "He rode on it. He played on it. He'd even strap a horse saddle across the hood and would ride a cousin around on it!"

TRACTOR RESTORATION

After nearly 50 years of faithful service, the dusty-and-rusty John Deere 4010 was assigned to a place of honor. Graceland decided, in 2008, to prepare the old tractor for display in the Elvis Presley Automobile Museum. Elvis Presley Enterprises replaced it with a new John Deere tractor and entered a cooperative effort with John Deere for restoration of the 1963 John Deere 4010. It included an agreement for future sales of die-cast replicas.

Nothing was typical about the restoration. Students at Northwest Mississippi Community College, along with instructor Shane Louwerens, restored the tractor with guidance from John Deere. At the college, only Louwerens and one administrator knew they were working with the original Elvis tractor. Students only learned the secret when officials from Elvis Presley Enterprises, Inc., and Deere & Company came to pick up the tractor and thank the students for their work.

The tractor was placed in a newly prepared exhibit space May 8, 2009, at the Elvis Presley Auto Museum on the grounds of Graceland.

Under the John Deere Ag Tech Program, Northwest College and Deere together offer training to develop entry-level John Deere service technicians. In the second-year special project class, students are required to work hands-on with broken equipment so they learn how to deal with the variety of problems they will see as John Deere Service Technicians.

John Deere's Atlanta (Georgia) branch contacted Louwerens to ask if he would be interested in preserving an old tractor with the help of students. Next, Louwerens's shop was inspected; he had no idea about the historic significance of the tractor being discussed.

"I felt like I was in a job interview at some prestigious company," he said. "They made sure our location was secure, and that we had the ability to do the project to their specifications. I was baffled when they asked me not to replace any parts unless absolutely necessary and any parts that were replaced had to be saved, bagged, and returned to them."

Then, only after Elvis Presley Enterprises decided that Northwest had the ability to complete the project, Louwerens was told the secret. Louwerens usually allows a few months to complete the special project. This time, he had 30 days to do the job. The students and instructor put 385 hours into the job.

Louwerens said, "Every one of our projects gets a nickname. We called this one Stella."

The tractor arrived February 17, 2009, shortly after lunch. It was in typical condition for a 1963 model. It required disassembly, pressure washing, and a great deal of detailed work. In all, only about 10 pieces were replaced. Some dents and scratches were left on purpose to preserve the tractor's historical and sentimental value. Students even used jeweler's polish to restore, rather than replace, the original gauges and light covers.

The students were required to keep daily journals of work performed on the tractor. Louwerens took photographs to document the entire process. For the collectors, his recorded serial numbers are for the tractor (4010 2 T 50686) and loader (E046A SN 10927).

John Deere and Elvis Presley Enterprises, Inc. licensed the Ertl company to make a highly detailed, die-cast, 1/16 scale replica of Elvis's John Deere 4010. The special edition replica is available at authorized John Deere dealers, at Graceland, and through toy-tractor dealers. Everything on the replica is "true to life" including the dents it acquired and even the unique 46A loader that is rarely found on die-casts.

Finally, the original John Deere 4010 "Elvis" tractor sits permanently displayed in a place of honor, bright, shining and polished for Graceland visitors to appreciate.

Tractors

BY BEN LOGAN

Novelist and filmmaker Ben Logan lives in New York City, although he remains rooted to the southwestern Wisconsin farm where he grew up. As he writes at the start of his colorful memoir of his family's farm, *The Land Remembers*, "Once you have lived on the land, been a partner with its moods, secrets, and seasons, you cannot leave. The living land remembers, touching you in unguarded moments, saying, 'I am here. You are part of me.'"

In this chapter from Ben's memoir, he describes his yearning for a tractor after seeing a Fordson at some friends' acreage in the 1920s. This story underscores the farmer's ambivalence toward the new-fangled tractor: part desire for the mechanical mule, part fear that it would symbolize the end to a way of life.

O ne summer when I was about nine I fell in love with tractors. It began with a Sunday visit of the whole family to friends who lived in a little valley branching off from the Kickapoo River. There was a boy my age named Don and an older boy named George. They also had two sisters and I didn't, so I was interested in sisters. But they told me sisters were a pain, and I took their word for it.

I envied Don and George even before they got a tractor. A little creek ran practically through their barnyard, the riffles filling the place with the sound of water and the feel of a long lazy summer day. There were suckers and chubs in the pools, waiting to be caught, and slippery mud puppies in the banks, looking like foot-long dinosaurs.

And on the steep hillside above the stream was a giant prostrate juniper that made a great ground-hugging circle of dark green. I had never seen a tree before that grew out along the ground instead of up toward the sky. It had decided to be different, and was a fairy ring that invited me to race around it in the short grass of the hillside until I dropped to the warm ground, panting and dizzy, breathing in the rich pungence of the juniper, feeling the hot sun beating down on me.

Those people had those two things, and they had a tractor. On this particular day we walked, Don and George and I, up the narrow valley along the singing creek to find the tractor. Grasshoppers flew up ahead of us, some of them landing in the water. We stopped to look down at a grasshopper thrashing in the middle of a quiet pool, sending out little waves in a perfect series of rings that vanished at the edge.

We argued awhile about whether the rings would ever end. If the pool were big enough, would they go on forever, maybe even after the three of us were dead? If the whole world were water, would the grasshopper waves go clear around it and meet on the other side? And where would that be? In the China Sea, maybe?

Then we argued about the grasshopper's swimming ability. For me to float and thrash my arms at the same time was a newly discovered and death-defying accomplishment. "He's swimming," I said.

"He's trying to swim," said Don.

We waited for George's opinion. He frowned down at the struggling grasshopper. "He's floating because he can't sink even if he wants to. He's trying to walk, like he was still up here in the field."

All at once the grasshopper wasn't doing any of those things. There was a little swirl, a sucking, crunching sound, and the grasshopper was gone. A bigger series of waves spread to the edge of the pool.

"He can too sink," said Don.

George got a patient, older-brother look. "He didn't sink. He was sunk. One of three things happened. A turtle got him, a trout got him, or a chub got him."

"Sometimes you sound just like a goddamned sister," Don said.

"You're not supposed to say goddamn," George said.

"You just said it. "

"That was only to tell you not to say it."

"Just the same you said it. And if you tell that I said it, I can tell that you said it, too. Anyways what about a frog?"

"I don't think frogs eat grasshoppers," George said.

During all this we chased down another grasshopper and threw him in the water. He drifted slowly downstream. Nothing happened.

"Let's go see the tractor," I said.

It was a Fordson with cleated steel wheels, a steering wheel of wood and iron, and a crank hanging down in front, the same as a Model T. It smelled of new paint, grease, and gasoline, and it crouched there in the hayfield, ready to spring into life. I walked around and around that tractor, seeing the heat waves dance up from the broad hood, moving in to touch it sometimes, then moving back and walking around again.

"How do you start it?" I asked.

"We can't do that," Don said.

For some reason we were both whispering.

George was looking back down the creek. A bend in the valley hid us from the farm buildings. George turned around and looked at Don. "Look, when Papa was using it up here yesterday, could you hear it? At the house?"

Don swallowed. "I don't think so."

George smiled. "Tell you what, little brother, if you won't tell I started it, I won't tell you said goddamn. O.K.?"

"O.K.," Don said. "I won't even tell you said goddamn twice."

George fiddled a minute with levers and knobs. Then he went around front and started cranking. The engine wheezed and coughed a couple times, smoke came out of the exhaust pipe, and then it started and settled into a steady roar. George climbed up to the seat, throttled it down, got it into gear, and ran it forward and back a couple of times. Then he stopped and waved me toward him. "Want to steer it?" he yelled.

I didn't know if I wanted to or not, but he reached down and helped me up to the seat. He got it going and stood behind me while I steered that vibrating monster in a slow circle.

George shut it off. I was holding on to the wheel so hard I couldn't let go. Slowly the sound of the creek and the flying bees came back. I finally climbed down to the ground. A bell was ringing.

"That's dinner," Don said.

We raced through the sweet-smelling hay, sending the grasshoppers, bumblebees, and honeybees sailing off in all directions.

That afternoon, driving back up to the ridge, I started talking about the tractor.

"You boys didn't start it up, did you?" Mother asked.

While I was trying to think my way out of that, Father saved me. He looked at Mother and said, "If you want a boy to make a habit of speaking the truth, there's some things you don't ask."

I wanted to reach across the seat of the Model T and hug Father, but then I thought about how that might say we had started the tractor. The moment of warmth passed.

Mother sighed. I knew exactly what she was thinking. Any time a bunch of women got together they talked about tractors as if they were some kind of monsters that roamed the country eating people. Those women had all the news for a hundred miles around about tip-overs, broken arms from cranking, fingers cut off in gears, and some poor man over in Iowa so chopped up and scattered it wasn't even worthwhile to buy a coffin. Some of it was true, of course. There was no arguing with the fact that one of our neighbors got confused and sat up there on the tractor seat pulling back on the wheel, yelling "Whoa," and drove right out through the end of the machine shed.

I read about tractors in the farm magazines that summer and talked about them until everybody was disgusted with me. The trouble was nobody else got excited about them except maybe Mother and Lyle, and they were on the other side. Lee liked the idea of getting the work done faster. Junior would have liked another engine to tinker with. Laurance dismissed the whole idea with such older-brother phrases as "just not a practical possibility."

Just mention the word tractor to Mother and she could see one tipping over, wiping out a whole family. Father listened to the talk and smiled, saying very little.

Lyle was the antitractor spokesman. I would bring up the subject and then it would go something like this:

"We don't raise gasoline. We raise hay. Ever try feeding hay to a tractor?"

"But a tractor doesn't eat hay when it isn't working."

"Doesn't make any manure either."

"But a tractor would save a lot of time."

"Sure, and what happens when you need a new one? We going to take the old one next door and breed it to a neighbor's tractor and wait for it to have a little tractor?"

It was no use. Lyle always got the last word.

Late that summer I was with Father when he stopped to talk to an old man named Abe who had a little farm out near the end of the ridge. Abe was standing at the edge of a hayfield watching a red tractor and a two-bottom plow roar across the field.

"Never thought I'd see a tractor on your land," Father said.

"Had to get one. My boy wouldn't stay with me otherwise. He's the last one I got. Damn it, Sam, a man gets old."

Abe picked up a clod of dirt and slowly crumbled it between his fingers. "I broke this land. This was the first field. I cut off the timber, grubbed out the brush. I put an old breaking plow behind three of the best horses that ever lived. I followed that plow around this field, dodging stumps, turning up rocks bigger than a man could lift. And goddammit, Sam, last year a man from the government was out here telling me I shouldn't be farming this hillside."

"You mean the county agent?" Father asked.

"Hell, I don't know. Could've been. It was one of those government men from somewhere. I told him it was the closest thing to a level field I got. Hell, he might as well tell me I should never made a living all these years."

The tractor roared by us in a cloud of smoke and dust, throwing up two fourteen-inch furrows of sod. Abe's son—I guess he must have been about twenty-five—waved down to us. He had a smile going that just about took up his whole face.

"He's got a glory all right," Abe said. "I had one, too. Mine was making this farm out of nothing. But that contraption—that's his glory."

"Well, things change," Father said in that way he had sometimes of just saying enough to keep somebody else talking.

Abe nodded. "Things change all right. That don't mean I have to like it. Seems to me a tractor gets a man up in the air too high. I figure I got to be down on the ground where I can get dirt on my hands and get the smell of it. I got to walk and get the feel of it under me. Then I can say when it's too wet or too dry. I can say what it needs. You can't tell me that boy of mine's going to know all that going across a field hell bent for election way up there on a tractor."

We left him there with a handful of earth running through his fingers, his eyes locked on the red tractor.

We got in the car. I was very quiet. Father looked at me. "What's the matter?"

It isn't easy when you're nine—or any age—to say you've thought of a man as being old and foolish and have suddenly found out he's not only not foolish but almost a poet of some kind.

"I didn't know he felt like that," I said.

Father nodded. "Still think we should have a tractor?"

I could feel the steering wheel of that Fordson jerking against my hands. I could smell the gasoline and hot oil smells and hear the roar of power I had commanded from way up on that swaying seat. I still wanted a tractor. But it wasn't the same.

"Not as much," I said. Father smiled.

Willowbee

BY GWEN PETERSEN

Gwen Petersen lives near Big Timber, Montana, where she raises miniature horses and works on her attitude. In addition, this Erma Bombeck of the barnyard writes a regular column for the *Fence Post*, performs at cowboy-poetry gatherings, and ramrods the annual Sagebrush Writers Workshop. She's also the author of two books of rural reminiscences, *How to Shovel Manure and Other Life Lessons for the Country Woman* and *Everything I Know About Life I Learned From My Horse*.

Your "first" tractor was an old-timer when you inherited it. A 1948 Ford. Purchased along with the ranch property, the little growler looked pretty spiffy. Gray hood and gray fenders swelling over fat black tires. Undercarriage and step-on fenders of bright red. Compared to the "BIG" tractor, this fellow stacked up like a Banty rooster compared to an ostrich. You decided it was a male tractor (it belched a lot and made rude noises and wasn't that easy to start). You named him Willowbee—you had and have no idea why.

In spring, Willowbee was often utilized for ditch cleaning if one first attached a blade to his rear end. You, of course, did no attaching chores if you could possibly help it. A female messing with a tractor was apt to receive a bite, a scrape, a pinch, a bruise or all of the above.

Therefore, the task of putting machinery parts together fell to your spouse, son, uncle, cousin, or a passing stranger of the male persuasion. Once tractor and blade were connected, Sir Spouse drove it along the irrigation ditches, blade angled to dredge out winter debris.

But Willowbee was an anomaly of the tractor kingdom. The old Ford actually kinda liked you—the mistress of the ranch. Because of his small size, you had no trouble climbing aboard. Possible reckless speeding didn't worry you as turtles could outrun the little Ford.

Come garden preparation time, you climbed aboard Willowbee, hooked the small spreader to his backside (well, Sir Spouse did the hooking) and trundled down to the pig sheds. Next to the corral rose a mound of straw and pig manure—the cleanings from the pens. You shoveled pig stuff—a pitchfork was the tool of choice—till your back protested too much. You repeated this exercise with horse droppings from the corral and chicken guano from the hen house. (The previous year your garden grew the biggest pumpkin and won the ribbon at the 4-H fair.)

Once you'd scattered the nutrients around the quarter acre garden plot, you viewed your handiwork and felt proud. The next step meant plowing. Therein loomed a possible problem. Though you and Willowbee had a mutual admiration relationship going, still, you preferred that your manly mate do the plowing. Why? Just cuz.

Dimly, you can remember a year when your beloved plowed the garden without being asked or hinted at. (You still treasure that memory.) When hints, demands, wheedlings, blackmail, and chocolate pie failed to get the job done, it became evident that your country man was not paying close—or any—attention to your requests.

Did you call him to an accounting? Of course not. You consulted your inner woman. You consulted Willowbee. The two of you came to an understanding. The morning your mate departed driving the BIG honkin' tractor and drill aiming to seed the South Forty, you took action. You grabbed your plowing cap (the one with the earflaps to prevent wind chill and earache) and leather gloves. (Experience had taught you that it was more difficult for a cranky machine to bite through leather.)

You saddled up Willowbee, plunked down on the iron seat and chugged down to the machine shed. In the far corner, underneath a mountain of old saved tires lurked what was known as—and probably still is—a two-bottom plow. (The term has nothing to do with the SHAPE of the plow. It means only that it's outfitted with two metal discs positioned on edge like blades of a giant pizza cutter.)

Flinging tires aside, you backed Willowbee within kissing distance of the plow. Now came the part where you employed your knowledge of the three-point hitch. First, you eyeballed Willowbee's hindquarters. A thick steel bar, called a drawbar, extended horizontally between two steel arms at about the level of your shins. The bar was secured by means of heavy bolts, which, in turn, were held by snap-ring cotter pins, or sometimes a fat nail and baling wire. You jerked sharply on the snap ring and pulled stoutly on the pin. Nothing happened except for a muscle separation in your upper arm.

Delving into the tractor's tool box, you pulled out a hammer. If the hammer had gone missing, you found a rock. With the pounding implement of your choice, you smacked the cotter pin and hit the bolt as well. You continued bashing until something gave and repeated the action for the other side. You stayed alert in case the loosened drawbar attacked. (If the drawbar leapt from its mooring and mashed your toes, you found yourself moaning at the bar.)

Once the bar was removed, you attached the plow by means of the same bolts and pins. Then you coped with something called a brace rod that was supposed to hitch from the small wheel of the plow to the axle of the tractor. Unsure of the hitching procedure, you avoided a problem by utilizing a piece of baling wire to secure the brace rod so it wouldn't flop on the ground.

When you had enough plow attached to yours and Willowbee's satisfaction, and the discs set in raised position, you mounted up and chugged toward the garden. In those long ago days, an irrigation ditch snaked twixt you and garden. Negotiating carefully across the ditch, you turtled up the short stretch of subsequent pasture and on through the back garden gate. You adjusted the level of the discs so they sank in only a little on the first round. You made a second round in the same track, only this time, adjusted the blades deeper.

In no time, rich black garden soil, blended with chicken, pig, cow and horse guano, turned its underside up. You sang merrily (a ditty of your choice) as you made the final round. Feeling like the Queen of Everything, you rumbled out through the garden gate.

Patting Willowbee on his steering wheel, you said, "Well done, Partner," put him in gear and started across that irrigation ditch. Oh, woe. Willowbee put a foot wrong. A wrenching jerk and his wheels bogged down in cold wet mud.

The tractor tilted and wobbled as if it had been imbibing boilermakers. As you slowly sank sideways you shifted into lowest gear hoping Willowbee would snort and buck out of the morass. Sadly, bucking and snorting proved unsuccessful and you discovered that to remain seated on the side-slipping machine required you to cling like a frightened monkey to the steering wheel. You gave up, slid off, crawled away from the bogged down Willowbee and returned to the house.

When seed-drilling master-of-the-homestead came chugging home on his BIG tractor, you had a tall, restorative drink a-waiting. Then you mentioned that Willowbee had taken sick and stuffed himself in the irrigation ditch.

You and Willowbee both survived and went on to other adventures such as checking cows during calving season. On the small Ford, you could drive up to and among the herd without stirring up any cow hysteria. And you had an eye-level view of bovines' southern exposures.

The morning you discovered a mama cow down and in birthing trouble, you dismounted from your steel steed and prepared to play midwife. This was a gentle older cow; you didn't feel any anxiety except about how to help her. Two little feet protruded. You took off your right hand glove, rolled up the right shirt sleeve and explored the birth canal. Egad. A breech birth. You didn't have calf pullers with you, but you did have an obstetrical strap stashed in Willowbee's tool box. Attaching a strap to each protruding foot, you sat on the ground and parked your feet on Mama Cow's rear. With her next contraction, you pulled mightily. That's when you discovered why upper body strength is a plus. Too bad you didn't have any of that. Sitting in the muck, staring helplessly, you cast about for another idea. The calf would die, maybe the cow as well if nothing could be done. You looked at Willowbee who stood by, saying nothing. But he looked sympathetic.

You guessed it. With minor adaptations, you hooked the obstetrical strap to Willowbee's draw bar, climbed aboard and gently gunned the motor to coincide with cow contractions. It worked. Out popped a nice bull calf. Putting Willowbee in neutral, you leaped off, grabbed the baby and made sure he had no material obstructing his breathing. You weren't paying any attention to the mama bovine. As much trouble as she'd had, you figured she'd stay down for a time. But then Willowbee coughed. He must have—because something interfered with your concentration. You learned what it was as a long low and menacing mooooo blew ripples in the air, not to mention snot.

You get go of the calf. Or rather you sort of heaved it in Mama Cow's face, flipped yourself backwards like a circus acrobat, clambered spider style onto Willowbee's tractor seat and shoved the shift lever into let's-get-out-of-here gear. Willowbee did his best, but irate Mama Cow, head down, eyes rolling, slobber flying closed in on his tail. She butted, nearly lifting the tractor off the ground. You bounced at least a foot up off the seat. Fortunately for both you and Willowbee, Mama Cow quit the attack and turned back to her baby.

Another walk down memory lane reminds you of the time Willowbee bent a gate into a pretzel shape. To be honest, it wasn't his fault. Entering and exiting the gate leading to the horse pasture was always a challenge if you were on the tractor. First you had to get down, open the gate, remount the tractor, drive through, dismount and shut gate behind you. The problem occurred during those moments when the gate stood open and the horses lingered nearby. An open gate to a horse is like Copenhagen to a snuff-using cowboy. Especially if the horses are colts or yearlings.

That afternoon, you and Willowbee had planned to take salt blocks to the pasture. You managed the dismount, open gate, remount, drive through, dismount, shut gate in spite of the group of happy equines nosing around. It's when you remounted that the trouble happened. You threw the gear into low—you thought. Now, in your old stick-shift pickup, you accomplished low forward gear by going from neutral to pulling the lever down toward your knee. On Willowbee, going from neutral and pulling the lever down towards your knee put him in reverse. You forgot that fact. When you yanked the stick and stomped on the gas, Willowbee lurched backwards, mashing the wire gate into an ornamental shape. He didn't stop backing till he'd reversed all the way across the lane and hit the opposite pasture's barbed wire fence post. Willowbee hadn't halted or even slowed because you had been rendered stupid with surprise and failed to remove your foot from the gas pedal.

When finally, the fog in the brain cleared, three horses had departed and gone on an exploring expedition. Though Sir Spouse did his best to repair the wire gate, it never got over a severe hunch in its midsection. Sir Spouse thought it was the funniest thing that had happened all week.

Willowbee's a whale of a lot older now. He is showing his age big time. In dog years he's about 400. Like you he sags in places he hadn't ought to, his skin is raddled, his feet are flat and he's gone blind in one eye. His tires are wrecked and digesting his oil and gas causes him heartburn. But he's up for one last chore.

Northwest of the house you've established your final resting place. An iron-railing enclosure with a view of the river and the mountains. You've made it clear in your will where you must be buried. But what about Willowbee? Is he going to be junked or maybe installed in a tractor museum?

Of course not. Your will instructs that Willowbee must be parked at the head of the grave as a tractor headstone. Let the elements rust him out, let time and weather sink his wheels into the earth. Let him, with his one good eye, survey all before him.

The cowgirl who's out on the tractor
Is happy except for one factor
When every last bump
Meets up with her rump
She's certain that someone has smacked her!

My First Tractor "Solo"

BY RALPH W. SANDERS

Ralph Sanders grew up on a central Illinois farm where he had ample opportunity to "exercise" regularly a 1933 Farmall F-12 and 1948 Farmall C. Helping neighbors bale straw, apply anhydrous ammonia, and shell corn also provided working acquaintances with a Farmall H, Farmall MD, and McCormick W-6.

Ralph became a journalist, working for *Prairie Farmer* and later, *Successful Farming* magazine. He is also the author and photographer of the long-running *DuPont Classic Farm Tractors* calendar as well as several thorough histories of farm tractors, *Vintage Farm Tractors*, *Ultimate John Deere*, and *The Farm Tractor: 100 Years of North American Tractors*, all published by Voyageur Press.

The challenge, that fine spring morning in 1942, was to drive our Farmall tractor by myself across the farm field, a distance of a quarter mile at the most. Pretty short trip! Simple enough, I thought. And I was anxious to do it. Dad needed to get both the tractor and our truck to the end of the field, without walking back to pick up the other vehicle. He figured I could "help" him by driving the tractor while he drove the truck.

My problem was, I had never driven the tractor "solo" before, and I wasn't sure I "measured up" to the task. I couldn't quite reach the clutch pedal…yet!

Sure, I could "drive" the tractor! I had done it many times before… but, with Dad sitting behind me on the steel pan seat of our 1933 Farmall F-12. Small at the age of nine, the tractor's foot clutch was still just beyond the reach of my left foot. I tried again with Dad watching. I just lacked the "stretch" to slide off of the tractor seat far enough to push down that elusive clutch pedal with my left foot…while clinging to the steering wheel for support.

So how could I start the machine from a dead stop and drive the Farmall across the field for Dad, if I couldn't reach the clutch pedal to put it in gear and then drive away? I was about ready to admit defeat. I was crushed by being too short to operate the machine by myself. My older brother Jack, at 12, was already driving one of our tractors alone…a skill he kind of held over my head.

WHERE THERE'S A WILL…

Dad, however, was not so easily discouraged. He showed confidence in my tractor driving abilities…even if I couldn't reach its clutch pedal. He had put in enough time on the seat behind me to know that I understood how the machine was operated.

"You can do this Ralph. I'll help. What we'll do," he patiently explained, "is, I'll get the tractor rolling for you, then I'll get off, drive the truck down there, and then I'll meet you at the end of the field to help you get stopped." He probably explained it a second time, because I remember him telling me that if I needed to stop the tractor for any reason, I should ground out the magneto with the kill switch located below the steering wheel. And yes, I assured him I could reach it. That would stop the tractor in its tracks.

So, seated behind me on the back edge of the seat, Dad adjusted the notched throttle on the right to a medium speed, put it in second gear, let out the foot clutch to get me rolling. Then he carefully dismounted to the ground at the rear by stepping off the wide drawbar. He quickly walked around the back of the left tire so he could check to see how I was doing. I was doing alright! I was heading south toward the field end as instructed. He gave me a thumbs-up signal, as he headed for the truck.

DEFINITELY NOT A RACE

With its three-speed transmission, originally designed for steel wheels, second gear was pretty slow, even after the transmission had been speeded up to better accommodate the use of rubber tires. Maybe I was moving over the field at 1 ½ to 2 miles per hour, so Dad had plenty of time to walk to our truck, and then drive it to our agreed upon common destination. Even at that snail's pace, I drove with careful concentration. This was important "work," I remember thinking. I held my course as straight as I could as I glanced around to see that Dad was soon underway through the field in the truck.

No, my path was not corn-row straight, but it was a decent track toward the power pole that marked our agreed upon meeting place. I had turned around just once for a quick glance to check my tracks. I was really driving, I reminded myself, feeling exhilarated by the experience.

ANOTHER SMALL STEP

Dad soon arrived at the field end and got out of the truck to meet me and the tractor in the field, safely short of the road. As he had earlier outlined, he walked from the truck to behind the tractor, deftly mounted the tractor seat behind me and brought the F-12 to a careful stop. I was tingling with excitement as he throttled down the engine to an idle. I did it myself! Just wait until I tell my brothers, I thought.

Dad and I exchanged smiles as we got off the tractor. Both of us were proud of our accomplishment that day. My feeling of self-worth was boosted by that small step. Dad had just put another facet to my interest in tractors...that of me actually using one of them for their intended purpose of farm work.

The Farmall model F-12, I first drove that day, was the second generation of a two-row farm tractor designed about 1924 to cultivate row crops, as well as to power most other farm chores. Its designer and manufacturer, International Harvester Corp., had earlier branded its row-crop capable machines as FARMALL, to better market the versatility of its design. The F-12 model was a smaller additional model to the then popular F-20 Farmall. The very first Farmall, introduced in 1924, later became known as the "Regular" model.

A young Ralph Sanders learns to solo on the family's Farmall F-12.

THREE FARM BOYS

Dad had three sons that he lovingly helped grow into productive young men by patiently teaching us how to work on the 250 crop acres on the Illinois farm. We also had three sisters, Mary, Becky, and Nina. Their attention was more focused at helping Mother at home and learning domestic skills. But, they also learned to drive our truck and tractors so they could help outside when needed.

In those early 1940s, when our country was fighting World War II, food production was given a high priority, and farm labor was almost impossible to find. So farm boys got to help at a young age. At least we did.

Brother Jack was the oldest son, and by the time I took my first solo tractor trip, he was already a competent 12-year-old tractor driver, and had already shown a preference for driving our model R-2 gas-powered Caterpillar. Jim was just a couple of years my junior, and was growing up fast. At the age of five, even before he started grade school, Jim had helped Dad combine soybeans one fall, by tending the 12-foot header on our 1929 model 36 Holt combine.

We had all three been able to handle the header job on the big pull-type combine. From the catwalk above the combine's header house, we were responsible for setting the header at the cutting height Dad signaled to us from his seat below on the Caterpillar tractor that pulled the rig.

A simple wheel, reminiscent of a ship's wheel, moved the header up or down in 1-inch increments. Most of the effort in moving the header control wheel was balanced out of the task by heavy counterweights near the end of long steel beams on the rear of the header. So, we lightweights could handle it.

Brother Jim was right behind me in learning to drive a tractor. But he learned his tractor driving skills on the seat of a new model 2N Ford-Ferguson tractor, which joined the Sanders' tractor fleet about 1945.

OUR LAST TEAM

In 1938, four years prior to my first Farmall tractor solo circa 1942, Dad had let me "help" him spread manure as he worked the farm's last team of horses, "Dick and Daisy," for a trade-in evaluation on that very tractor. During those intervening four years, the little row-crop tractor had proven its usefulness on the farm. The two-row Farmall had adequately replaced the team of big Shires. And, fulfilling an uncle's prediction, Dad was indeed to raise three sons who didn't know a thing about horses. We never did learn to harness or handle a team. The Farmall F-12 had replaced the last team on our Illinois farm. And our farm generation were soon tractor drivers instead of horse handlers.

RUBBER TRACTOR TIRES

Dad had improved the Farmall with new knob-tread rubber tires replacing its original steel-lugged wheels. A step-up transmission gear from International Harvester soon boosted the tractor's three operating speeds to take advantage of the new faster rolling pneumatic tires. College trials in the 1930s showed about a 20 percent gain in useable horsepower for rubber tires compared with earlier lugged steel wheels with which tractors were first equipped. Rubber tired tractors also could save up to 25 percent of the fuel used by the steel shod versions. It made sense for Dad to convert it to rubber tires.

During those years while World War II raged overseas, rubber tires were rationed and scarce. So it must have been through special wartime farm food production exemptions and special permits that Dad acquired and had the new tractor tires installed.

HARROWING EXPERIENCE

My first field-working experience with the Farmall came about a year later than my first "by-myself" trip. It was probably in early spring of 1943 at the advanced age of ten that I did my first actual field work. I remember the experience vividly.

Spring-plowed ground, like on our farm's heavy soils, often needed to be harrowed down with a four-section spike-toothed harrow soon after it was turned over by the moldboard plow. That kept it from drying out and forming hard clods and losing too much moisture. Harrowing was a job the Farmall and a boy could handle. In the meantime, I had grown the few inches I needed to finally reach the clutch pedal and had become a full-fledged tractor operator.

Dad got on the tractor with me for the first few rounds on the 20 acres or so of fresh-plowed ground that needed dragging. He showed me where to drive to work the soil the full width of the harrow without either overlapping or skipping spots in the field. He helped me set the pitch levers on the harrow sections to do the best job in the fresh-plowed soil. Then he turned the harrowing over to me and he went back to plowing farther west in an adjoining field. "If you have any problems," he said, "stop the tractor and come and get me."

I resumed harrowing and was getting more comfortable with the work when it happened. At the north end the field I was turning the tractor and harrow around to make another pass through the field. Busy making a sharp turn, I was watching the inside harrow end to assure that it left no "skip" as it turned, and didn't notice the harrow hitch start to rub the back of the inside rear wheel. In short order the hitch was riding up and onto the tire. I finally heard the hitch bumping on the tire tread and glanced back. By then I had a real mess back there! I did a panic stop, took the tractor out of gear, and then throttled down. My heart sank and my legs trembled as I got off the tractor and looked at the broken hitch still perched about halfway up the back of the tire. I figured I was in deep trouble!

Dad had seen it happen from his tractor seat, and got to me before I reached him. Instead of being angry with me, like he had a right to be, he was calm.

As he sized up the damage he quietly asked, "Do you know what you did wrong, Ralph?" "Yes," I meekly admitted apologetically, "I turned too short." He suggested that I could fix that problem by glancing back at the implement during the turn. And, he further suggested that I could throttle down during the turn to give myself more time to keep everything in control as I turned on the end rows. Lesson learned! He was even more patient and careful with his sons as he was with his farm machinery.

BALING WIRE PATCH

Next I helped him straighten out the piled-up harrow and size up the damages. He then patiently patched the broken two-by-four hitch evener with baling wire. It wasn't good as new, but it would work. Almost all of our farm machines carried several strands of used baling wire…always handy for a field patch job. That too was another good lesson in field expediency repairs.

And then I climbed back up on the tractor and continued my harrowing until the plowed ground was all smoothly harrowed down. Even with the little Farmall, a four-section harrow covered a lot of ground in a short time. I think that day's lesson stuck with me. I don't remember ever piling up a harrow again. I later thanked my lucky stars that the tractor had been changed to rubber tires. Had that harrow hitch caught on a steel wheel spade lug, it could have really flipped that harrow on top of me and the tractor.

"MY" TRACTOR

The grey F-12 Farmall with its red wheels soon became "my" tractor when we boys and Dad went to the field to work. Yes, our 1933 model was painted gray...not red. International Harvester began painting all of their tractors red, starting in 1936, a couple of years before the F-12 was replaced with the improved model F-14.

"JUMP-JUMP" FOR STALKS

That tractor helped me grow up during the following eight years. After school and on Saturdays, I was soon planted on its non-cushioned seat, chopping and discing corn stalks following the fall harvest. A straight-bladed two-row rolling stalk cutter hitched to the tractor drawbar, pulled a 7-foot single disc behind it. We nicknamed the stalk cutting rig "Jump-Jump," for the bouncing action the cutter imparted to the tractor. The straight blades jumped the rig down the corn rows as each blade impacted the ground. The cutters of more sophisticated design had enough of a spiral built into each blade to even out its ground contact, so they merely rolled, instead of jumping, down the field like ours did. The jumping stalk cutter was an economy model bought through Sears, Roebuck and Co. and their David Bradley line of implements.

CLIPPING STUBBLE

Of the two attached implements that came with the Farmall F-12 tractor in 1938, I used the rear-mounted PTO-driven sickle-bar mower the most. The other implement, a front-mounted two-row cultivator, Dad used for cultivating corn. Without benefit of a power lift, Dad was the only one of us who had a strong enough back to lift the cultivator at the end of the row.

Dad was then still following a classic four-year "permanent-fertility" crop rotation of corn, soybeans, wheat, and clover. With the clover or other legume spring seeded in the winter wheat, the wheat stubble needed to be clipped after wheat harvest in July, to give the legumes some light to get established before frost. That's where the Farmall and I performed our "dance." The fresh-cut wheat stubble was the stage. The mower's cutter bar, I think, was 7 feet long. When conditions were dry, you could mow in third "high" gear at full throttle. We might have moved as fast as 5 mph. For the F-12, that was fast as it went.

Perfectly turned corners called for skill in rapidly whipping the tractor 90 degrees to the right and then just as suddenly straightening it out to resume the mowing. Done just right, the cutter bar would back out of its cut in the outside corner, and then swing back into the new cut leaving a neat right-angle corner. A touch of righthand brake applied in the turn slowed the right wheel to a near stop as the left wheel raced ahead to complete the turn. A "spinner" mounted on the four-spoked cast-iron wheel made the rapid turns possible. I provided the power steering.

"COW PIES" SLOW PLOWING

Dad sometimes pastured the standing rotational legumes with our milk cows and feeder steers. After standing over for a growing season, the legumes were plowed under the following spring to be planted to corn to begin the next four-year crop rotation. Spring plowing soon turned the clover field black. It was a task our three tractors and growing young drivers usually attacked as a team.

The F-12 boasted about 12 horsepower at the drawbar. On rubber tires it was a little stronger than that. That figured out to a plow capacity of two 12-inch plows. Dad bought a used pull-type with two 14-inch plows for the tractor to pull...just a bit too big to for it to handle under all conditions. But the 14-inch furrow it turned made it compatible with the four 14-inch bottoms pulled by our Caterpillar R-2, and the mounted two-bottom 14-inch bottoms on the 2N Ford.

I could usually just keep up with the other two tractors as we three brothers plowed together on one "land." What could stop the F-12 in its tracks, and throw my brothers into fits of laughter, was when the Farmall's land wheel encountered a fresh "pasture muffin" and spun out. Deft application of the left handbrake to transfer power to the furrow wheel, usually got the rig rolling again, and back into the plowing race.

"ARMSTRONG" STARTER

Like other farm tractors of its era, the Farmall was started by turning over the motor with a crank. For small boys, that could be quite a chore. As we grew in strength and stature, cranking got easier. We decided that we were "men" when we could crank the engine continuously, or "spin" it. We were either "men," or the poor little tractor needed a ring job and had lost most of its compression.

WAR YEARS AND MORE

"My" tractor, the aging F-12, served the farm well for more than ten years from 1938 to about 1950, when it was finally traded in on its replacement, and I got a new tractor to drive. The new tricycle type Farmall model C was a row-crop machine of the same two-plow power category as the F-12. The shiny red machine was up to date with electric-starting, lights, and hydraulic controls for its mounted implements. All it lacked was power steering.

Dad ordered the new tractor with the two-row front cultivator, rear-mounted sickle-bar mower, and a front-mounted two-row planter.

I enjoyed working with the model C Farmall during summer vacations, especially cultivating soybeans and corn. I left the farm in 1954 for military service, followed by college, marriage, family, and a journalism/photography career. I didn't go back.

Today that "new" C, which replaced "my" F-12 tractor, sits in the corner of the farm shed on the home farm in Illinois, awaiting the day when someone will restore it as an antique to pay homage to the fine old machine, and to the growing boys who became men working the farms of our great country, more than 60 years ago.

Love at First Sight

BY SCOTT GARVEY

Scott Garvey is a world-renowned expert in the field of tractor archaeology. As the author of T*he Tractor in the Haystack: Great Stories of Tractor Archaeology*, published by Voyageur Press, he told the stories behind dozens of fascinating tractor finds.

A writer and photographer, he is also a regular contributor to the world's largest tractor magazine, *Classic Tractor*. He is based in Saskatchewan, Canada.

The thing about growing up in a family of farmers is I experienced a lot of tractor firsts. Not just on the farm I lived on, but on those of neighbours and other relatives, too. That left me with many great memories of different models over the years. Despite that, my recollections of one particular machine stand out. That is because when it comes to tractors, just like in life, you never seem to forget your first love.

In the 1960s and most of the 1970s, my grandparents lived about four miles down the road from our farm. And unforgettable days spent there are among my earliest recollections of first encounters with some very memorable tractors.

My grandfather had a particular fondness for Minneapolis-Molines. Before he decided to take up farming, he owned a small-town garage with a franchise to sell those yellow tractors. After he sold the garage and moved to the farm, he kept his preference for them; he even brought a couple with him to work his fields.

In all, he had four model Us. Two of them were working tractors and two were parked on a hill at the back of the yard—at least for as long as I can remember. The hill was the spot where his old tractors were put out to pasture, figuratively and literally. Tractors that ended up there had only one remaining job: to sacrifice their parts when one of the working models suffered a breakdown.

However, one of those hill tractors—the better one—remained in running condition for a while. It was parked there only because it was equipped with steel wheels. For several years it was left mostly intact. This machine had done the lion's share of the work opening up new land for cultivation in the first few years after my grandparents arrived. Occasionally, I can remember that tractor being started up—with some effort— and used as the cultivated acres were expanded. That meant clearing large stands of trees.

The steel-wheeled tractor was ideal for use on the "new" land, because the first few cultivation passes were pretty tough going. They were so tough, in fact, that a rubber-tired tractor was at risk of getting a flat. After a bulldozer pushed the trees and brush into a pile, tree roots and broken stumps were left littering the field. They could be murder on tires.

Once those first few passes were made, the steel-wheeled U's job was done, and the rubber-tired models took over. By then most of the stumps had been laboriously picked by hand and hauled off the fields. That meant the steel-wheeled U could rejoin the parts tractor on the pasture hill at the back of the yard.

Riding that steel-wheeled machine was no picnic. The steel wheels transferred every bump directly to the driver. The rubber-tired models were a little more comfortable, but anyone who has spent time on tractors built in the 1940s and 1950s knows comfortable is a relative term.

The steel seats on the Us weren't even state of the art when those tractors rolled off the factory floor. They were, however, a standard feature on most tractors of the time. But even a quick look at seats in cars and trucks of that era should have offered a clue to tractor engineers that there was a better alternative.

Maybe the steel seats remained popular with farmers because they were cheap to produce and helped keep tractor prices down. That would appeal to farmers, who have always been known as a practical and thrifty bunch; and for the most part they still are. My grandfather certainly fit into that category. He was about as thrifty as they came.

He certainly wouldn't have sprung for the extra cost of a fancy seat on his yellow Us, in spite of the fact he felt the steel seats were uncomfortable. But not in the way you might expect. To him, a tractor was better off without a seat, entirely! In fact, he went so far as to completely remove the seats from both of his working tractors and the steel wheeler. When he spent a day behind the wheel, he would stand on the steel platform where the seat would have been.

With their low rear platform, the Us seemed ideally suited for a standing driver. I'm not sure if that is what designers had in mind when they first sat at a drawing board and sketched out the initial prototype, but it definitely worked to my grandfather's liking.

On most tractors, removing the seat would have made working the clutch impossible; but the Us had a hand-operated version, which, once again, seemed to have been designed for a standing driver.

Although, the logic behind a tractor without a seat escaped me. Even as a youngster, the idea of spending a day driving a tractor while standing up seemed nuts. But what did I know?

However, other members of the family shared my opinion, and grandpa was the subject of a seemingly endless running joke about his seat-less tractors, even years after he retired from farming. But he shrugged off the criticism with a good-natured smile. Thinking back, I never did get a reasonable explanation from him that fully accounted for his hatred of steel tractor seats. Maybe the cold Canadian winters had something to do with it!

And thinking about it further, it couldn't have been because he found them completely uncomfortable. He did put them to use. One summer day, he retreated into the farm workshop with the seats, an armful of scrap pipe and a few disc blades from an unused discer. A little while later he emerged with his new invention: a set of steel-seated lawn chairs. He welded the seats to the end of a piece of steel pipe and used the disc blades as a base for them.

He proudly placed them under the shady trees near the house and relaxed on them with a cold drink on hot afternoons; he no-doubt needed to sit down after spending all day standing on the tractor. As far as I was concerned, there was a time and a place for steel tractor seats; and that wasn't one of them. The regular canvas lawn chairs were much more comfortable.

As years went on, I spent a lot of time around the old Us; and my grandfather eventually decided he would teach me how to drive them. Under his guidance, I learned how to engage a clutch, albeit with a hand lever. I would later have to translate my perfected smooth-engagement procedure to a foot pedal.

In the process of learning, though, I popped the front wheels of the U off the ground a time or two. And I can actually remember knocking my grandfather off the rear, standing-room-only platform during my first clutching attempt. I had a firm hold of the steering wheel and the clutch lever, so I was able to stay on board. Fortunately he avoided being run over by whatever the tractor was pulling at the time. Undaunted, he persevered and directed his young protégé to try again.

In the end, engaging a clutch was a feat I was more than a little proud to have mastered. After that, my grandfather occasionally trusted me to stand up behind the wheel and drive the Us around, taking care of a few simple jobs.

But despite being a lover of all things mechanical—especially tractors —and having perfected my hand clutch technique on a yellow Minneapolis-Moline, I never really did share my grandfather's passion for them. They were OK, and some of the design lines were pretty classic and well placed, at least that was my considered opinion as a pre-teenager. But, I always thought they lacked something, aside from a seat.

Maybe it's just that it was the '60s, a decade when new and modern things were in fashion; and old things were out of style. The Us were old, even then.

Later in that decade, I was able to put my finger on exactly what was missing from the old Us. The realization came to me on one memorable afternoon. That day when I arrived at my grandparents' farm, grandpa had just taken delivery of a brand new, square-fendered 830, J.I. Case tractor. This machine was nothing like the old Us. The new Case had exactly what the old Us lacked—modern styling, and a foot clutch!

The 830 looked like a giant compared the old M-Ms. Knowing how he felt about those yellow tractors, I'm sure my grandfather would have much preferred to have bought another Minneapolis, but by then that was no longer possible. They were long since out of production; and the company, itself, no longer existed. But probably the biggest and most practical reason he had for purchasing a Case was there was only one tractor dealer in town. And they sold—you guessed it—J.I. Case.

When I first saw the Case parked in front of my grandfather's tractor shed that day, it was love at first sight. The shiny new tractor required an urgent and close inspection, which I promptly gave it. I liked everything about this machine. I don't know who was responsible for the styling of that tractor series, but in my estimation then, and now, he hit a home run with the design.

Sitting on the seat of the Case and surveying the view from up there was like sitting on the top of the world. I sincerely hoped Grandpa was going to leave this seat firmly attached where it was; it felt more like an armchair than anything remotely resembling those old steel seats on his homemade lawn chairs. Clearly this tractor offered a new generation of creature comforts; that put it in a completely different league than the old yellow Us.

And the Case had diesel power under the hood, unlike the gasoline engines in the older tractors. The throaty rumble of the Case's diesel seemed so much more befitting a farm tractor. This thing spoke with authority!

There was so much about this new tractor to like. Whenever we went to my grandparents' farm, I had to climb up onto the 830's seat and just sit there daydreaming about being in command of it. I could imagine some kind of tillage implement following behind and a little black smoke coughing out of the exhaust, just enough to show the tractor was putting in an honest day's work. That thought seemed as pleasurable then as dreaming about being in control of a Boeing 747 in mid-flight might seem to some today.

Back in those days, no one thought twice about taking a rider along on a tractor; fenders and cab interiors weren't plastered with warning stickers reminding operators not to do that, like today's models are—except for those tractors with their own built-in buddy seat for just such a purpose. And when I was a kid, I spent more hours riding along on tractors than I did looking out the window of the school bus. But getting a chance to ride on the Case was always something special.

And one of the memories that sticks with me to this day is sitting on top of the big, left-side, square fender of the 830, which seemed then to be about as large as the deck of an aircraft carrier. I was about 12 at the time. My grandfather was at the wheel as several of us baled hay on his farm.

I can remember my father and younger brother riding on the hay wagon behind the baler; they were lifting bales off the long chute behind the New Holland 273 baler and stacking them on the wagon. Maybe part of the reason I remember this is because I had spent more than a few hours riding the wagon under the hot sun stacking bales myself, so riding idly on the tractor was something of a treat in itself. Farming back then was hard work, even for 12 year olds. But being on the Case is central to my memories of that day.

The 830 felt like a friendly giant as it slowly made its way down hay swaths; its diesel rumbled along easily as the tractor swayed slightly from the motion of the baler's plunger, which swung back and forth as it compacted hay into tight bales.

But I suppose it's really one of those times when you're together with your family that makes mental images like that one so special, and the tractor itself seems as familiar and important as any family member. In fact, over the years many of us have spent nearly as many hours with a particular tractor as we have with some of our real family members. Small wonder tractors feel more like old friends and coworkers than mechanical machines.

A few years later, my father borrowed the Case to power a used model 42 John Deere pull-type combine that he bought one fall. My grandfather had a self-propelled combine, so the 830 would have been sitting idle for a few weeks anyway. The new-to-us combine wasn't all that big, but it was too much for our IH Super W-6, which didn't even have live power take off. So if the combine was going to swallow any wheat, it had to have a little more tractor in front of it than the old International.

The Case had no trouble delivering enough muscle, and harvest on our farm that year was moving ahead much more efficiently than it ever had. Then, trouble. A faulty water pump bearing on the 830 let go, allowing the fan to inch forward and slice into the radiator. Needless to say, after that delay combining dragged on late into autumn.

The next season, my father purchased a 3020 John Deere which took over the "heavy" work around the farm, including powering the pull-type combine. By then I was 15, and old enough to be given responsibility for doing field work with it. And that led to another one of those memories of my grandfather's Case.

One summer, Grandpa was getting behind in his cultivating work, and he needed a little extra help. So I was sent to his farm with the 3020 and our cultivator to help him catch up. My grandfather and I spent a day working side-by-side cultivating one of his fields. It turned into a kind of a competition. He and the Case against me and the John Deere.

Although he definitely had an edge in the horsepower department with the 830, we had comparable loads with our cultivators; he had a 15-foot model, and I had 12 feet behind me. We raced against each other to see who could cover more ground. The odds were against me, but I came up with a plan to make up for my disadvantage. Grandpa was going pretty deep and really ripping things up. I inched my smaller 12-foot cultivator up a little making a shallower draft, which made for an easier pull. I geared up, let the John Deere cough out a little smoke and really turned over some dirt.

Looking back, I don't know exactly how cunning that plan really was, but it seemed like a stroke of genius at the time—I hate to lose. Knowing Grandpa, he probably went out the next day and reworked everything I'd done to get it exactly to his liking. He was a perfectionist.

At the end of that day, though, we decided to call it a draw. We'd each covered a lot of ground. And I think he enjoyed the day working beside his grandson much more that he let on.

When my grandfather sold his farm, the Case, the last remaining U able to move under its own power, and all the rest of his machinery was sold by auction on a cool, late-fall day. Seeing the tractor go off to a new owner was a little sad, but by then there were several newer and interesting machines on our farm, so my infatuation with the Case had faded into the background a little.

But as years go by, the early memories we all collect have a way of coming back to haunt us. Those of us whose lives have been so intertwined with machinery always seem to maintain an unshakeable interest in the equipment—particularly the tractors—that first held our attention so many years ago.

In fact, a similar sentiment with automobile enthusiasts has motivated manufacturers to release retro versions of some popular cars. Now, even the tractor manufacturers are getting on board with the idea, hence New Holland's introduction of an 8N Ford tribute model. So far, though, no 830 Case.

Where Grandpa's Case eventually ended up is anybody's guess. It's one of those tractors I'd love to find—if it's still in one piece. But despite the fact I've resigned myself to the notion I'll never knowingly see it again, I have found a replacement for it.

About 15 years ago, when I came back to farming, my father knew I needed a tractor of my own. He happened to be at a local farm auction sale when a good-looking 930 Case was failing to capture any interest from the crowd. He raised his hand when bidding stalled at about half of what the tractor was worth, then everyone else washed their hands of it and the auctioneer said sold.

That day the 930 came here to its new home and went straight to work. It lacked the air conditioned cab that all of my neighbours had on their newer machines at the time. But it proved to be a reliable workhorse just the same.

Even though other tractors have since come and gone on this farm, the 930 still lives and works here; but not because it remains indispensable to our operation. It now spends more time sitting in the yard waiting for a job than it does hard at work. Sitting on the 930 in the open air is a pleasure on nice days, but the air conditioned cab on the newer tractor makes life a lot more pleasurable when spending a long day in the field.

What it lacks in creature comforts, the 930 makes up for with its timeless styling. It has the same elegant design that inspired love at first sight when I saw Grandpa's 830 as a wide-eyed, 10 year old. That has to count for something!

I just don't think I could part with the 930. Even though it's surrounded by much newer, easier-to-use, and more fuel efficient models, driving it does something operating the shiny new ones doesn't: it brings back fond memories. Memories like sitting on the fender watching my grandfather as he drove his 30-series tractor.

Country Music Star Michael Peterson's First Tractor

BY JOHN DIETZ

Raised in Richland, Washington, Michael Peterson is well known for his million-selling country music tunes as "Drink Swear Steal & Lie" and "From Here To Eternity." And he's been nominated several times for Grammys and Country Music Association awards.

Some of Peterson's inspiration comes from an unlikely source—a small, blue Ford tractor. Here he tells his tale.

A little blue tractor is a pretty reliable place for musical inspiration, says Michael Peterson. It's new in his career, and only a small part of his globetrotting life as entertainer, composer, music producer, but it is a very special place where he's composed quite a few songs.

Michael Peterson has been composing, singing, recording, and producing music for about 30 years. He's stepped away from the floodlights

Michael Peterson's *Down on the Farm* CD.

of high-energy country music entertainment and moved in his own direction. He's a family man, a minister to servicemen, an encourager to communities, and a musician.

Michael Peterson had a meteoric rise to the pedestal of American country music in 1997 with his first album. *Billboard Magazine* recognized him as the top selling new male artist and top new airplay artist in 1997–1998. His million-selling country music chart toppers from those days ("Drink Swear Steal & Lie" and "From Here To Eternity") are still popular with both nearing the prestigious 2 million airplay mark in late 2009.

In the four years between 1997 and 2001, the country music star did more than 700 performances around the globe and had five consecutive Billboard top 20 hits. He also was nominated for Grammy and CMA awards.

Then, while they were still 'playing the daylights' out of his tunes, Peterson just got off the road. For reasons which have been unclear until now, he changed direction. He pulled back on touring, switched record labels, reduced his public profile.

"My growing sense of being 'off purpose' led to a significant decrease in my public profile and became a catalyst for my decision to reset my target on what I am now calling 'Purpose Driven Artistry,' " Peterson said for this report.

FIRST TRACTOR

The roots of the man on the tractor go back to Arizona. He was born in Tucson in August 1959. His father had a PhD in hydrology and worked in the atomic energy industry; his mother was a homemaker. The family moved. Michael grew up in the tri-cities area of eastern Washington, close to Richland, where the Columbia River meets the Yakima River. He wasn't a city boy, or a farm boy, by any means. The area, like central California, is very dry, arid, desert-like, and distinguished for producing high quality irrigated grains, fruits and vegetables.

"I had a great childhood. I remember the banks of the Columbia River, big wheat country, hops, and barley. It was both a farming community and a government nuclear energy facility community. We were surrounded by both. You were either connected to the government or involved in farming. Most of the people who were there were either doing something directly related to that or supporting that. We liked to joke, 'that's why the apples were so large'. It was a great place to grow up," he said in an extended telephone interview.

Before there was a tractor in his life, Peterson recalls a mix of music on radio, ranching, and 4-H activities. It's a "vague memory" as to why he joined the high school 4-H Club. "You get choices about what you want to take in high school; somehow that appealed to me," he said. Somehow, too, he became president of the club. Other interests, in those first days of high school, were horseback riding, guitar lessons, and football.

At West Richland, a friend of the family owned a little working ranch agreed to give guitar and horse-riding lessons to the 14-year-old in exchange for weekend ranch help.

"That's probably when I saw my first tractor," Peterson said. "She had a quarter-horse and an Arabian named 'Igor'. I worked on her place, bucking hay and cleaning up. I started taking riding lessons from her and learned how to play guitar."

One of his closest friends lived at a second ranch in West Richland.

"We bucked a lot of hay a couple of summers in a row, when we were 14, 15, 16 years old. His dad would give us a couple bucks an hour to go out and throw hay bales onto a hayrack."

Music and football were major elements of daily life for the future Nashville star.

"Growing up, country music was all over the radio. I grew up on Charlie Rich, Freddie Fender, Willie Nelson, Merle Haggard," Peterson said. "In the mid- and late 1970s, an awful lot of country music was being played on Top 40 radio. Freddie Fender's song 'Wasted Days, Wasted Nights,' was a top pop hit. Merle Haggard's 'Okie From Muskogie' crossed over to the pop charts. Charlie Rich had crossover hits, 'The Most Beautiful Girl in The World' and 'No One Knows What Goes on Behind Closed Doors.' Dolly Parton had 'Nine to Five;' Kenny Rogers had 'Islands in The Stream.'

"A lot of country music was crossing over to the pop charts, and showing up on KALE, the local radio station. It never seemed an odd thing to me to enjoy Merle Haggard and Led Zeppelin. It never seemed odd to me that you could listen to an Eagles tune and, also happen to like the Oak Ridge Boys. You could hear it all. We loved popular music, and a lot of it was country."

The record collection in his grandmother's house was another source of inspiration. He spent many hours listening to those records at her house.

"She had this huge record collection. She loved music and exposed me to the standards. It definitely wasn't the kind of music my friends were listening to, but if it hadn't been for her, I might never have found Cole Porter, Harold Arlen, or Hoagy Carmichael," Peterson told an interviewer for the Country.com website.

Michael Peterson began singing in high school and church, whenever and wherever he had the opportunity.

"I think I was a performer first, a composer later. I had an aptitude for music more than I had an aptitude for algebra. It just seemed to come a lot easier to me," he said.

"When you're a young person, you look to discover who you are, where you fit and what you're good at, to find some encouragement. I found a lot encouragement around music. So I started off just being a singer, trying to get a solo in the choir, hoping I'd be good enough.

"We had a great choir teacher at high school, named Ted Bear. He had a great music program, with several performance choirs."

But music wasn't Peterson's only interest. Being 6' 4" tall and having natural athletic ability, Peterson soon was involved in athletic programs. His closest friend, David Flaherty, was an all-star wrestler, and a musician.

"We and a few other guys seemed to have a foot in the music lane and a foot in the sports lane. We seemed to be able to straddle those lanes."

As high school graduation approached, Peterson was offered scholarships in both football and music at Pacific Lutheran University. He chose both, but eventually gave up the music scholarship to focus on football.

Peterson started for 2½ years at Pacific Lutheran as left offensive tackle. Pacific Lutheran rose in the football ranks to win a national championship. The starting quarterback, Brad Westering, another man with a foot in both music and sports, became a close friend.

CAREER VISION

Looking back on it, Peterson said, even as he moved into the football track, another vision for his future career developed.

"My dad passed away in my senior year of high school. On the heels of that, I found this album by an artist named Dan Fogelberg, 'Netherlands'. It really spoke a lot to me about life and about the value of life.

"I remember thinking, as I was heading off to university as an 18-year-old freshman, that this man's music moved me so much that, if I could ever write songs like that, I'd like to. I think, that's why I started to write songs, just to express the grief I had over losing my dad and some of the things that had happened in my life."

The football jock, in those college years, found that music was an effective way to express his feelings. He started writing songs, continued playing guitar and singing, whenever he could.

"People seemed to like what I was doing, even as basic as it was at 18, 19, 20, 21, 22 years of age. The more I did it, the more I felt I liked it; the more I liked it, the more I created, and it seemed like, the more response I got from people."

About three years after college graduation, Peterson got a call from Westering. It opened the door and really settled his career direction. From here on, Michael Peterson had both feet in the music lane.

Westering had become a music producer. He enlisted Peterson to write songs for rhythm and blues/gospel singer Deniece Williams. The success of Williams' new albums led to new contracts for the rising songwriter. One of his new songs in 1993, "Taking Your Love for Granted," was chosen by an old-time Christian gospel group, The Imperials, for a new record. It became a hit among fans of contemporary Christian music.

" 'Taking Your Love for Granted' became No. 1 and, with that song, the Imperials became the only group in history to have No. 1 record in four consecutive decades," Peterson said. "I'm actually co-producing an album for them now, in their sixth decade, and have several songs on that recording. Funny, how things turn out."

Peterson spent the next two or three years building relationships with Nashville songwriters. He told Country.com, "I can hardly explain to you how wonderful it was for me to be able to work with and, in a few instances, become friends with writers who had been my heroes. People like Dewayne Blackwell, Gene Pistilli, John Bettis, Jim Weatherly, and last but not least, Josh Leo and Robert Ellis Orrall. The education I received working with those people and many others created an explosion in my hunger and growth as a writer."

Collaborating with Leo and Orrall, Peterson's songwriting blossom-ed. In one concentrated period, between October 1995 and June 1996, Peterson wrote or cowrote about 70 songs. Several were cut by other art-ists in the next months, but with the help of Orrall and Leo, for the first time Peterson recorded some of his music and found a label that would release it, Warner/Reprise.

Michael Peterson, his self-titled debut album, was released in June 1997. It generated five top 20 country music hits and led to international recognition. For about three years, he was the "toast of Nashville."

However, the second album and those that have followed revealed the "real" Michael Peterson.

BEING HUMAN

Michael's second Warner Brothers release, *Being Human*, was quite dif-ferent. Peterson described it in a 1999 Billboard interview as very emo-tional, very intimate. He said, "It really moves from the joy of taking bet-ter care of yourself to the joy of taking care of someone you love." The release was condemned by one critic for having "relentlessly upbeat lyr-ics." Peterson actually took that as a compliment; it was right on target.

He was committed to creating commercially viable music, but he was on his own path. He was focusing his intentions on writing good songs and, more importantly to him personally, using his talent and time to offer help for people looking for encouragement.

As a songwriter, Peterson continues to develop music for others as well as himself. He has written songs recorded by such Grammy winning superstars as Travis Tritt, Timothy B. Schmit from The Eagles, Deniece Williams, The Classic Imperials, and more.

As a performer and entertainer, a decade after *Being Human*, he con-tinues producing new CDs and has a unique road program.

Peterson brings music and encouragement to American service members on overseas duty and at home. He has visited bases in Iraq, Afghanistan, Korea, and Alaska several times since 2005. As National Spokesman for the American Legacy Scholarship, he has performed for the American Legion National Convention every year since 2005. He was also keynote speaker at the Global Leaders Conference at West Point Military Academy and at the 2008 National FFA convention.

A four-year tour sponsorship with New Holland allowed him to co-create innovative promotions for the agricultural industry. The New Holland tour allowed him to entertain and remind large audiences across North America that modern farming is all about strategic value, innovative brilliance, and committed stewardship, consistently delivered.

Separately, in school programs, a new generation is meeting Michael Peterson. His national tour, "My Real Life, Strong for America," brings the artist for a week at a time into contact with schools and communities. A concert ends the weeklong visit, but the focus of the week is on meeting needs, on sharing stories, on motivation.

"Strong for America" has three goals: to help students who are looking for career and educational direction, to help adults invest time and talents in their community, and to help leaders and retirees find ways to strengthen the community. It aims to leave a legacy, a program that will endure to the continuing benefit of each community visited.

LIFESTYLE FARMER

Back at home, there's a lawn to mow. He and his family reside on eight and a half acres in a Nashville suburb. They moved to the acreage in 2001.

"Some might consider me a lifestyle farmer," he said. "I've got about three acres that are open, that look more like my front lawn. I've got a pond that covers about an acre in front of my place. It has some catfish, bass, sunfish, and snapping turtles. The house has a large Victorian wrap-around porch. There's a lot of woods. It's a very picturesque place.

"I had somebody else taking care of all my lawn work for the first five or six years that we lived here. I was on the road a lot and didn't have time to do this. We had a riding mower that really wasn't meant for a big place like this. I think I went through a couple of those, beat the daylights out of a couple of inadequate vehicles, before I realized I needed something substantial."

His current tractor is a two-cylinder, hydrostatic, New Holland Boomer TZ25DA subcompact equipped with rollover protection, a front-end loader, and a mid-mount mowing deck. It arrived in July 2007, but it wasn't his first tractor. He had enjoyed the use of a similar model for a year while doing promotional work for New Holland. The little, but "substantial," yard tractor does much more than keeping the lawn pretty and getting the artist off the couch.

"Somehow I manage to get on the tractor six or eight times a year and mow my acreage. It takes me four to five hours to mow the place."

Even before the current tractor arrived, in November 2006, Peterson agreed to serve as the national spokesperson for the Childhood Agricultural Safety Network. Backed by a coalition of health and safety organizations in North America, the campaign in 2007 and 2008 led to promotion of safety awareness for farm children on hundreds of television and radio stations and in more than 100 agricultural trade journals, newspapers, and newsletters.

Advocating for child safety around tractors was a natural outgrowth. He knew the power of the tractor he was enjoying, but Peterson also has two girls growing up and has had "a couple of accidents with machinery" over the years.

"I come from a place of understanding how quickly something can happen. I took a tumble on the tractor I currently have. The tractor stalled and left me sitting up on a bank a little bit sideways. I thought I had enough brake to hold it. I put it in neutral, and it started rolling down the hill. I wasn't hurt, but I know that in the blink of an eye, man, something can happen," he said.

Kids and mowers just aren't a good combination, according to Peterson. He advocates, and personally practices, keeping children away from machinery until they're old enough to be trained as operators. For his own clear conscience, he insisted that his girls stay away from the mower until he had a chance to "really show it to them and teach them about it."

As it happens, neither of Peterson's daughters is interested in driving the tractor, and he's OK with that. He remains the primary user of the tractor. The yard is beautiful. The tractor is a big part of helping keep it that way.

However, since the real yard tractor arrived, Peterson has changed.

"I mow my lawn with it on a regular basis now, and I really enjoy it," he said. "When I was a kid, my Dad liked to work on the lawn. I never understood that, didn't understand how it could be relaxing for him, but I'm older and I get it now.

"It's not work. It's something not related to the facts, figures, things that many of us do for a living. On a tractor you're outside, riding around. You can look behind and see what you just did. There's a sense of immediacy about the payback."

PLACE OF INSPIRATION

For an artist, he explained, riding the tractor for hours at a time is inspirational. He collects notes about good ideas on a computer, but the tractor has become a place where the creative juices turn those ideas into words and melodies.

"Quite frankly, I like sitting on my tractor. I have written a lot of songs, riding on that tractor. I'm working on a song about Texas right now. The last time I was mowing, I wrote probably three-fourths of that song. Another song that was written while riding that tractor was called, 'That's What They Said About The Buffalo.'

"I don't know the science exactly, but when you put the body in motion doing something that is a learned habit, like riding a bicycle or driving a car, it tends to free up the creative part of the mind in a way that you might not find if you were just sitting down and trying to be creative.

"I try to find those spaces, and riding on my tractor has been a great place for that. It's because you have the hours."

It's All in the Thumpin'

BY PHILIP HASHEIDER

Philip Hasheider is a writer and farmer. He's also the author of several guidebooks to farming, including *How to Raise Cattle* and *How to Raise Pigs*, both published in cooperation with the FFA. His articles have appeared in many newspapers, including the *Wisconsin State Journal* and the *Wisconsin Academy of Review*.

A former cheesemaker's assistant, he lives on a farm near Sauk City, Wisconsin, with his wife and two children.

It's not an understatement to say that the magic of a John Deere could grip a teenage boy's imagination in ways no female form could. You could talk to it, you could caress it, and it responded to your beckoning any time of the day. If the color of love for a young farm lad was green, it involved a John Deere, or in my case, our John Deere Model G. Love is blind and the rusty coat it wore made little difference; it was a real beauty in my eyes.

The G wasn't the first tractor my dad owned but it is the earliest memory I have of any on our farm. My loyalty to it remains even though it eventually took up residence on a neighboring farm, and my ties to it are but a distant memory; I long for one more ride.

Our Model G was the Rodney Dangerfield of John Deere's tractor roster. Like the comedian of ironic self-deprecation, it did all the work but didn't get any respect. But boy, I loved that tractor. It was known as a dual-fuel tractor, using gasoline and distillate/kerosene, with two fuel tanks; the smallest one located nearest to the forward steering column. Yes, it burned lots of gas, had slow hydraulics, and the wheel width was so hard to adjust that Dad finally set it for thirty-eight inch corn rows and left it there for the rest of the time it was at our farm. Oh, and did I mention that it over-heated a lot, once so badly it cracked the head? It was a brute; heavy, hard to steer but, in classic farming parlance, it could really pull.

The G was part of Deere's string of alphabetical tractors, added to their line in 1938 and promoted as the thirty-five horsepower row crop answer to their preceding A, B, and M models; all efficient but with diminished power. By 1952 John Deere abandoned their confusing alphabetical labeling for a numbered system of increasingly more powerful machines.

To a pre-teenage farm kid, that special magic radiated by tractors could be found in unexpected places such as our county fair. Many farm equipment dealers displayed machinery at the fair every July, and on the last day they held tractor parades; each dealer sitting proudly on their tractors, showing off their latest models as they snaked their way along the dirt tracks.

It drew crowds—huge crowds—because a lot of farmers came to the fair. Some came to see the 4-H projects, some for the vast amount of machinery on display, and others who, if they needed an excuse, used it to the full extent of having a day off the farm.

One year after the machinery parade ended, the John Deere dealer put one of his tractors in motion by locking the right wheel brake and then positioning the steering so that the left wheel kept driving, turning the tractor in a circular, clockwise direction. Then he dismounted from the rear and watched as a crowd gathered around.

I stood, peeking out from behind my dad as we watched this amazing perpetual motion machine spinning in circles. The crowd grew but kept a safe distance as they gingerly crept up to watch this tractor revolving around itself, like a dog chasing its tail.

Their initial wonder quickly turned to nervous laughter, followed by more than one farmer taking a slight, tentative step back as the tractor growled its way past them. The riderless machine continued digging its way round and around and seemed to pick up speed on each rotation, fueled by an internal anger, goading itself on. The stationary right tire sculpted a slightly deeper hole into the sandy soil with each turn while its mate chewed a circular path.

Mothers deftly pulled their children back into the crowd as black smoke belched from the stack, the racing motor determined to unleash itself from an invisible collar. They recognize danger when their husbands often are blinded to it. A mother's instinct knows unpredictable things happen on a farm. They sensed what would likely happen if that single brake unlocked, and having their child run over by a loose, abandoned tractor was not their reason for attending the fair.

The owner finally was satisfied with the effect of his novel idea had on the crowd he drew and climbed back on, timing his grasp of the seat rail with the tractor turn. Once on the seat, he pushed the clutch to stop its motion, unlocked the brake, and straightened the steering. Then he put it back into gear to let the tractor claw its way out of the fresh hole, and finally turned off the engine.

The crowd dissolved as quickly as it had appeared. He sat on his tractor, alone on a metal island and watched the sea of human curiosity wash back with the tide into the fair carnival. He seemed pleased as he got off and walked over to us. He obviously knew my dad because he called over using his name, "Hi, Howard."

They talked but nothing more was said about his tractor although my father was grinning. Finally, bursting with impatience I blurted out, "How did you do that?"

He looked down at me through his thick glasses filmed with the dust churned up by the tractor tires. He just smiled and appeared to cast a wink of his eye towards my father before turning back to me saying, "Well, I just gave it a little thump with my knuckles and it did the rest. It's all in the thumpin'." And he snapped his wrist with the outstretched knuckles of his index and middle fingers into the air, imitating how he cast a magic spell over his John Deere. That seemed fair but when I tried it on our G later at home nothing happened. All I had to show for it was a pair of bruised and skinned knuckles and a tractor that didn't move.

The G got the brunt of our farm work—plowing, planting, discing, and chopping; even silo filling. This tractor signaled a change in the history of our farm. By the late 1940s, my dad had bought it to replace the registered Belgian work horses that had powered the farm from my grandfather's youth in the early part of the century. Grandpa loved his horses, having owned several imported from their namesake country, and was a master at handling those ton-weight animals even though he stood only five foot four inches and tipped one hundred fifty pounds dripping wet. If he could make those gigantic horses mind his commands, he had no problems with grandchildren.

Nostalgia was not my grandfather's long suit. Perhaps because he became fatherless at the age of four and together with his young mother and four older sisters and brother, they worked two farms. Tomorrow's meals were never secured by looking at yesterday. Grandpa readily adapted to steel horsepower.

The G was Grandpa's favorite tractor. Maybe because the clutch was easy for him to use because it was engaged by pushing forward a long lever on the right side of the steering wheel rather than by a foot pedal found in later models. The shift lever for reverse or the four forward gears was positioned within an iron shell on the foot platform and was maneuvered around the five slots that resembled the teeth of a carved pumpkin. When the clutch lever was pushed forward it set the tractor in the desired direction. The throttle was located just above the clutch and confusing the two could create an alarming and dangerous situation for the driver as it was known to jump from the sudden and unexpected acceleration. Finally the G became too much even for Grandpa to handle in his later years and he finally relinquished it like he did his beloved horses.

The G powered the silage blower, which was belt-driven off the pulley located on the right side of the tractor frame, just ahead of the rear wheel. Silo filling would test its full power capacity. Wood blocks were often placed in front of the rear wheels because the torque created by the belt pulling against the spinning blower paddles loaded with silage increased the effect of pulling the brake-locked tractor towards it. It was a massive tug-of-war between two groaning, stationary machines with only the straining, spinning belt between them.

My brother made a habit of filling the blower hopper with as much silage as it would hold just to make the G work hard. As it struggled against this increased load, the front end would begin to bounce like a bronco straining to dislodge its unwanted burden. Black smoke shot up from the muffler as the engine labored and, with such maximum capacity stress placed on it, there is little wonder the G eventually overheated.

And it overheated a lot; once so badly that it cracked the head. Dad didn't want to fix it but our local dealer found a new engine head in Iowa, and Dad felt he had better because Grandpa still drove it. When the refurbished tractor came back, the new head was the only true green part remaining; the rest of the tractor's paint had worn off long before.

The G had two top stacks near the front that were a curiosity unique to that model. When viewed from the front, they formed a surreal letter H of a kind that Salvador Dali might have created had he designed tractors. I thought it was part of Deere's plan to spell out the next alphabet letter until my brother explained that one was a muffler and the other the air intake.

Two six-volt batteries powered the electrical system and were located under the seat. Twin batteries were used because the twelve-volt single units, still in their infancy, were unreliable. The tractor lights were never used, at least not on our farm. Partly because the batteries weren't powerful enough and partly because when it got dark, we quit the fields until the next day. That's a simplicity lost with the air-conditioned, satellite-linked, stereo-encapsulated cockpits of today's massive tractors.

"Go get the G, will you?" Dad said to me one day when I least expected it.

There was an unspoken directive contained within that question; get the tractor and drive it over to where he was working and don't ask why.

This was the first indication that Dad considered me capable of handling it by myself and I was going to make the most of it. My chance was no different from what other neighbor farm boys my age had. We'd compare notes at our country grade school to see who became the first to do things; driving, discing, plowing. It became a quiet contest of who did what first. Being the youngest in my class, I always came in last.

By this time there weren't any farmers left near us who still used horsepower; the four-legged kind, not those compressed into a steel frame run on rubber wheels. They had slowly disappeared although some still roamed the rolling hills having literally been put out to pasture, if they had survived at all.

But now I raced across our farmyard to jump on the G before Dad could change his mind, forgetting his warning not to treat a tractor like a toy. A father's advice can be forgiving; a mistake with farm machinery is not. I scrambled up and plopped myself on the hard seat and realized that this was my chance, alone and without Grandpa as bodyguard or navigator.

When riding with our grandfather, it was either sitting on his lap or holding onto the side fender. The left fender was used because most of the equipment was pulled off-center to the right; the combine, the plow, the hay mower. We—my older sisters and brother—were never allowed to ride on the right side fender. Mostly, I suspect, because if we fell off we would get into the path of the equipment, and besides, standing there hindered Grandpa's view as he watched the machinery over his right shoulder. There was no riding when the disc was used because the disc blades tracked wider than both rear wheels.

When Grandpa drove it, he would sometimes make motions like he was still driving his horses down the row. Occasionally he'd let out a call which I guessed had some meaning for him. Maybe he missed his Belgians more than he let on. But he always paid attention to what was happening around him, a far cry from my absent-minded wanderings, watching the rows or watching the birds following in the wake of the plow, scooping up worms.

One time when riding along with him, the left wheel hit a huge clump of dirt as he plowed and caused it to pop up off the ground, catching me off balance and almost throwing me from the back of the tractor. My seventy-five-year-old grandfather grabbed my shirt before I could even grab the fender or I might not be recalling it now. By holding me tight, he steadied my legs, and he did this all while maintaining his grasp of the steering wheel with his other hand. Now I knew the iron grip his horses felt when they failed to heed his commands.

He never spoke of it again; not to my dad, not to me. Perhaps he never thought of it again. But I did and it flashed through my mind like a laser now as I grabbed the steering wheel to drive it over to Dad.

Dad's request was like a pardon or a sentence lifted because I had finally reached the age of twelve. He had established this age as being old enough to drive a tractor alone, but it was our mother who made sure that rule was strictly obeyed. A mother's directive is not so forgiving.

It seemed an arbitrary age and while I was jealous that my brother crossed that line sixteen months before I did, nothing I could do—no begging, no cajoling, no simple asking could change that rule. I was told they didn't want me to have an accident. I never heard of any fatal farm tractor accidents in our immediate neighborhood; the lost hand, fingers, various limbs, sure. However, when machinery accidents did occur, the effect was immediate and the news spread quickly. For several days following a rare accident, a knowing silence descended on each farm as the spared families took extra care when working with their machinery. That caution, too, soon dissipated and work was back to normal.

But now it was finally my turn. My feet barely reached the left brake while I switched on the ignition. I had watched them start it many times so it should have been second nature for me, except I had never been allowed to do it myself. Now in my excitement, I had failed to pull the full forward throttle back but had instead pushed the clutch lever forward. When I pushed the foot starter, I was quickly confronted with the consequences of my mistake as the ignition engaged and the engine accelerated. The last thing I remembered hearing was my dad yelling, "Don't . . .," but the rest was quickly drowned out as the G lunged forward.

I panicked and pushed the foot brakes, trying desperately to stop it, instead of pulling back on the clutch or throttle which would have. The last driver had left the choke pulled out and black smoke coughed from the muffler. With the tractor sputtering, I held tight to the steering wheel thinking of nothing else, oblivious to my dad's hollering.

As it lurched forward, the front end lifted as the sudden engine acceleration and forward gear movement merged like a snorting, angry horse rearing on its hind legs with its rider holding on for dear life.

I clutched the steering wheel so tight that my fingers turned white. Suddenly the tractor stalled and bounced to a stop, like air escaping a collapsing balloon, and I was left sitting where I started only moments before, a relative sea of calm released from the gripping chaos of motion.

I must have looked a ghost when Dad scrambled up beside me. I was still clutching the steering wheel with a determined look but with tears in my eyes realizing this might be the last time I drove alone for quite some time. I turned and looked up at Dad, who towered over me next to the seat. He put his hand on my shoulder and gave it a gentle shake. He stood there breathing hard from running. Without saying a word, he was quietly taking in what he had just seen.

A mixed look showed in his face—part chuckling, part worried, and part afraid my mother would find out. Finally he laughed, reached forward, rapped his knuckles on the metal housing in front of the steering wheel and said, "It's all in the thumpin', isn't it?"

Learning the All-Important Mechanics of How Tractors Work

Pa oils the wheels of Junior's first tractor while Spot tries to help in this Deere advertising painting by artist Walter Haskell Hinton.

Junior tries to start the Deere, using his strength on the flywheel. *Library of Congress.*

Pa shows Junior the details of the family's Farmall's controls.

The famous 4-H book, *Tom Brent and his Tractor*, which taught thousands of kids how to care for their families' machines.

Junior wins an award for his 4-H tractor maintenance efforts.

Abishag

BY ROBERT N. PRIPPS

Bob Pripps was born in 1932 on a small farm in northern Wisconsin, and developed an infatuation with things mechanical at an early age. Through the years he worked with many different makes and models of tractors and crawlers, and earned his private pilot's license by the time he graduated from high school. Bob became a flight test engineer on the RF-101 Voodoo, and later worked on Atlas missile base activation for General Dynamics and jet engine starter and constant speed drive testing for the Sundstrand Corporation. But through all of his mechanical interests, he has remained faithful to tractors.

After retiring, Bob began writing a book on his favorite tractor, the Ford. The book, *Ford Tractor*, was published in 1990, teaming Bob with renowned English automotive photographer Andrew Morland. Since then, Bob has authored more than a dozen seminal books on classic tractor history and restoration.

Abishag: (Hebrew) King David's beautiful concubine brought in to keep him warm when he was "stricken with age." 1st Kings 1:3

My first tractor, a 1946 Ford-Ferguson 2N, was acquired from a private party in 1989. Owning a Ford tractor was the fulfillment of a boyhood dream. Owning it also led me to my second career (after retirement from the aircraft industry) as a writer of books on tractor lore. What I didn't know about tractors, including Fords, when I bought the 2N could have filled a book. Nevertheless, this tractor, which I named Abishag, has pretty well lived up to my expectations.

When I retired from my engineering job in the aircraft industry twenty-two years ago, I knew that I would need a remunerative activity to supplement my retirement benefits, at least until Social Security kicked in. I cast about for various business ventures that did not require too much capital, and one that would not tie me down to a regular work schedule (after all, I had just given up a job like that). I had already started harvesting maple syrup on land I'd inherited, so expanding that was an idea. I acquired the Ford-Ferguson ostensibly to help with the syrup operation.

With the acquisition of the Ford tractor, it soon came to me that it was a very interesting and historically significant piece of machinery. So I decided to do some research and try my hand at writing a book about it. I turned in the rough manuscript in 1990 to Motorbooks International and they were interested. They teamed me with famed automotive photographer Andrew Morland. The result was *Ford Tractors—1914 to 1954* published in 1990; the first of some twenty-five books I've written for them since; eight of them about Ford tractors.

In the late 1980s, very few people considered the N-Series Ford tractors to be collector items. Almost all were busily working on small farms, airports, and golf courses. Gerard Rinaldi was publishing his *9N-2N-8N Newsletter*, doing his best to get the little gray tractors some respect. Gerard put me in touch with Palmer Fossum, one of the first big Ford collectors. Andrew Morland and I visited Palmer and got many of the photos for that first book. I also learned more Ford tractor lore from Palmer than I had acquired in months of research. Palmer, who had become a close friend, passed away in 2007 at the age of 80 years. The auction of the remnants of his collection took place in October of 2009 and took two full days of hard selling to complete.

Bob Pripps' first tractor arrives at his maple syrup "ranch" in northern Wisconsin in 1989. The little Ford-Ferguson had been painted "new blue" by a dealer in 1964.

What makes the Ford tractor so interesting? First and foremost, the three-point hitch set the tractor apart for about the first 10 years of its existence. After the patent restrictions had been opened to competition, all surviving tractor makers adopted the concept. Secondly, I found the little tractor to be remarkably tough, serviceable and handy, more so than newer, larger types from other manufacturers. Until the advent of the small Japanese diesel tractors (costing much more) the N-Series Fords were virtually alone in their class.

The boyhood dream aspect began in about 1946, at the age of 14. The father of my boyhood chum, Earl, got a new Ford-Ferguson and implements for his 80 acre farm. Earl's dad also worked an off-farm job; so much of the routine field work was left for Earl. How lucky could a kid get? My envy was in no way satisfied until at age 50, I was able to get my own 1946 2N.

Earl and I are still buddies—Now I have a Ford-Ferguson and he doesn't. Somehow, and I can't understand it, Earl does not seem to be as envious of me now as I was of him then.

The 1939 to 1952 Ford-built tractors had a profound impact on the agricultural industry. Their configuration and three-point hitch sounded the death-knell for the big, heavy, low-powered row-crop tractors of Ford's competitors. Despite this, the little gray tractors never got much respect (as Rodney Dangerfield liked to say) at least until many years later. Even today, as most Ford N tractor enthusiasts know, the tractor public at large tends to lump them all together. Just recently, for example, I stopped at my local Kubota dealer to ask about a fairly straight 2N he had on his used-tractor lot. I asked him what year it was. His reply: "You mean the 9N? It doesn't matter, they're all the same." Some, but not all, recognize the differences between the 9N-2N and the 8N, but I've run into people who call them all "Fordsons."

When I first acquired Abishag, the 2N, I also got a nice back blade in the deal. With that, I made most of the trails through the forest for access to the maple trees for gathering sap. Over the years, there has been a succession of sap-hauling tanks for it. Even now, when we gather most of our sap with plastic tubing, there still are a few buckets to be gathered where tubing runs are inconvenient. Later, I've added a lifting boom, a buzz saw, a snow blower, and a logging winch.

In my job in the aircraft industry, I was involved mostly with either testing or marketing. In both cases, writing reports and sales proposals was a normal part of the duties. The proposals, sometimes, got to be "book length and size," so writing was not new to me. For research for the first book I had, of course, my experience with my 2N, and a couple of Ford Tractor manuals supplied by Ford-New Holland. I had also made a trip to the Henry Ford Museum and Greenfield Village. Next I acquired an I&T Manual and a book by Michael Williams, an Englishman; it was mostly about Fordsons, however. On a trip to Washington, D.C., prior to my retirement, I had the opportunity to visit the Library of Congress for further research for that first book. What I found there was that I pretty much already had everything printed about Fords in my possession, and that wasn't much. Thus, the visit to the Palmer Fossum's farm and collection was a Godsend!

Interestingly, another good friend that I have made as a result of writing these books about Ford tractors is Mr. Harold Brock. The 94-year-old (at this writing) Mr. Brock was the chief engineer of the tractor projects at Ford from 1938 to 1956, and is the primary "horse's mouth" authority on the Ford tractors of the time. Mr. Brock knew personally Henry and Edsel Ford, Henry II, Harry Ferguson, and most of his team, Thomas Edison and Harvey Firestone. Also interestingly, Harold Brock's first wife (who died after Harold's retirement) worked in the Ford headquarters office and knew Henry Ford personally, as well. Some time after she had passed away, Harold made a trip to Detroit on behalf of the Society of Automotive Engineers (SAE). He visited his old offices and became reacquainted with Kathleen, the lady who became his second wife—she also had worked in close proximity with Henry Ford and his associates. After the death of Henry Ford and under the leadership of Henry II, things in the Ford tractor business changed markedly. In an effort to be among the first to bring a multiple-speed power shift transmission to market, marketing forces overwhelmed engineering restraint. Harold insisted the transmission needed much more development and testing than it had thus far received. At loggerheads with management, Harold left Ford and finished his career at John Deere. The John Deere power-shift transmission was an unqualified success. Ford tractors initially delivered with the "Select-O-Speed" transmission had to be recalled and rebuilt with a later version of the transmission after much further testing and development.

Some say Harry Ferguson and his team had as much to do with the birth of the Ford N-Series tractors as did Henry Ford and his team (Harold Brock disputes this, however). Ferguson's main input was his early development of the hydraulic three-point hitch. Ferguson had teamed with the British company, David Brown, to produce a small tractor with the three-point hitch, called the Ferguson-Brown. This tractor's performance was impressive, but high costs kept sales down, and low sale kept costs high. Ferguson knew the expert on mass production was Henry Ford. In early 1938, Ferguson demonstrated the traction and maneuverability of his Ferguson-Brown tractor at Ford's Fair Lane Estate. The result was the famous hand-shake agreement between Irishmen Ford and Ferguson, wherein Ford would mass produce tractors with the Ferguson system and Ferguson would organize a dealer network and build implements. This arrangement worked well enough as long as old Henry was alive. After his death, Henry II realized that Ford Motor Company was losing money on every tractor produced. Thus, in 1947, the handshake agreement was abrogated. Ford went on to build and sell tractors without Ferguson, and Ferguson went on to build similar competitive tractors under the "Ferguson" brand name. My 1946 2N was built in the next-to-the-last year of the Ford-Ferguson arrangement.

In 2004, I delivered Abishag to N-Complete, Ford tractor experts and rebuilders in Wilkinson, Indiana, for a complete "remanufacturing" job. After a month or so, I returned to pick her up. She was beautiful! The paint job was far better than that done at the factory, and everything, except for the cast iron parts, was new. The cast iron parts had been inspected for being in "new" condition, meeting new-part tolerances. So, after 58 years, Abishag had a new lease on life. If she lasts another 58 years, I'll be—let's see, how old…?

Bob Pripps pilots his 1946 Ford-Ferguson 9N during the Michigan Wilderness Tractor Ride in 2006. The caravan traveled for forty miles daily over two days with nights camping out. Pripps' tractor had been "remanufactured" in 2004.

How Could a Grown Man Be Nuts About Old Farm Tractors?

BY CHUCK BEALKE

Chuck Bealke writes a monthly web blog chock full of his remembrances of growing up on a farm entitled "Life on the Farm." His family farm was located west of St. Louis, and raised a range of crops, including soybeans, wheat, corn, and hay as well as Polled Hereford cows.

Some background may explain why I am so fond of tractors and working the land. When I was 12 and living in town, my grandfather died and left his farm in Chesterfield, Missouri, to my mother. It was a beautiful place with rolling hills, pasture and woods, and I had spent many weekends there while growing up. No machinery came with the farm, and when my family moved from city life to the farm a year after my grandfather's death, my dad had it farmed by others while he continued to drive to his job in St. Louis.

I befriended a farmer who worked some ground owned by the private high school I attended (actually jumped onto his drawbar while he was plowing one day) and started working for him every moment I was not in school or studying. I fell in love with farming and tractors. I particularly liked moldboard plowing (in fact, still do and crave it every spring). The farmer, Erwin Sellenriek, who farmed his own land as well as what he rented, taught me well. It was heady stuff for a 12-year-old—driving a powerful machine and producing a fine seed bed in (usually) lush fields. My work was both enjoyable and valued. The fields were scenic and alive. My companions were crows, hawks and other birds with occasional visits by foxes, rabbits, blacksnakes, plowed-up gophers and such. I also learned to fence, butcher (hogs), combine, grade and plow snow from roads and lots of other things.

The first two summers while living on the farm I worked for the same school where I had met Erwin, mostly sickle-bar mowing with an early AC B and a John Deere H. I continued working for Erwin and became intimately acquainted with bales. Figured out loose hay, too, by working for a neighbor (Joe Blank) who farmed with a team (a Belgian and a Percheron) and filled his big barn with enough hay every summer to feed them all winter. I became fast friends with Joe, who was as fine a man as any I've known, and later named my first son after him. Joe loved the fields, his life in them, his creator and his fellow man. In his later years he switched from horses to a tractor, but he missed his team for a long time when he did. But Joe got attached to his tractor, too. It was a fine Farmall Super A with a Woods mower.

All the money made from working during my 13th and 14th summers went to buy a tractor—my first. This was earned by hot hours of tractor mowing, yard work, and some hay bale wrestling for others. I went to two farm auctions and bid on Farmalls and a Ford at the end of the second summer. At these sales I stayed next to a farmer I had worked for to ensure the auctioneers took me seriously. I came to know my heart better by the pounding it did as I put in my highest possible bids at the auctions. It was definitely scary-thrilling to wager two summer salaries in one whack. I did not get any of the auction tractors, but heard of a better deal after the second one. A friend of a friend found a Massey Harris 44-6 at Lonedell, Missouri. I made an offer to the dealer who had it (the entire salary sum saved) and got it bought and delivered quickly.

Talk about walking tall! For ye not acquainted with the breed, a 44-6 was a fair sized tractor with a six-cylinder Continental Red Seal engine. It was bigger than the Farmall H, AC WC, and lightweight Ford 8Ns that I had been working with. My Massey was about as big as a Farmall M—in my young mind a real man's tractor. The only reason that I was able to afford it was that it lacked hydraulic power and did not lend itself as well to adding same. (I later came to be a mini-expert on all the available ways to add hydraulics to such tractors, but none of them proved satisfactory.) Somehow I scraped up enough money to buy an old disc later and talked a neighbor who had just bought a Ford 8N with a mounted plow into letting me use his old rope trip plow. Presto-Testo—I had a way to start working ground.

The 44-6 proved a gentle giant, but the lack of hydraulics did a lot to build up my arms when my dad bought a sickle bar mower for me to use in mowing our farm pasture. It also limited my snow clearing capability to that afforded by pulling some kind of wooden triangle or other such contraption. This was not much of a threat to heavy, wet Missouri snow. Before our farm road was paved, I used the 44-6 to pull an old horse drawn road grader with big hand wheels above it (cranked forever to position the blade) to grade the crown down to level. To swell my head a bit more, the neighbor who I borrowed the plow from also came to fetch me a few times to pull a really heavy wagon load from another farm up his steep gravel drive. His 8N tractor would just sit and spin on the steep graveled hill that was his farm entrance and not budge the load. My Massey would spin just a bit over the rocks, but would pull a good load right on up the hill from a stop.

For a pre-driving age guy, I was enjoying working with a big machine. Of course, this was despite the fact that the 8N could mow circles around me in a field of heavy hay due to its hydraulic lift—especially if there were gophers or trees in the field.

Your first tractor is like your first girlfriend in that you tend to remember her well years later. The days I spent with the Massey left the rolling fields looking trim and ship shape and me with a sense of accomplishment. I still feel lucky to have been outdoors farming in such beautiful country with such a fine machine of my own choosing.

Reflections of the Fifties

BY ELLIOTT DOMANS

International Harvester enthusiast Elliott Domans writes for a website devoted to the small-yet-great Farmall Cub. His reminiscences of his first tractor—as well as his current restored tractor—is indelibly tied back to his life growing up on a farm.

I remember growing up in the 1950s in a small, rural town in northwestern New Jersey. The closest town to ours was only 3 miles away, and there were seven dairy farms in the areas of this and another country town.

We had 5 acres, and because my dad was a salesman and not a dairy farmer, he let the Bockovens, who owned the Willow Tree Dairy, farm most of our land.

One of my earliest farm experiences as a young boy was running into the back field, as Don Bockoven and his dad Frank were making hay. Don would cut the hay with a sickle bar mower attached to his 1946 Farmall M, while Frank pulled a side delivery rake with his 1948 Case row crop.

My sisters and I, and our neighborhood friends, used to play in the hayfield, making trails and pretend forts just before the hay was tall enough to be mowed. When that time arrived, we knew we could count on getting a ride on the hay wagon, and help with loading the bales of hay. The best time of all was riding on the hay wagon down the hill to the farm where we would help unload the bales onto a conveyer that carried them up into the hay loft of the huge red barn.

Life was so simple then; none of us realized how complicated things would become over the next twenty or thirty years! The roads in our town were gravel, and one was even still dirt then! Cars had running boards, and occasionally we'd get to ride on the running boards of the neighborhood cars coming back up the hill on West Main Street from the center of town. We would hold on to the center door post with the front and back windows rolled down, and away we would go at the break-neck speed of 25 or 30 miles an hour up the hill on the running boards of Frank Dean's old '38 Chevrolet.

The Willow Tree Dairy was where my family got our milk, and every morning Don Bockoven would get into his 1952 Divco milk truck and drive his milk route around town.

The glass quart bottles of milk were kept in a large cooler. They were iced down with cold well water and block ice, and somehow Don always knew how much ice was going to be enough to keep the load of milk cool on a hot summer's day. There was always a generous supply of cream at the top of each of the milk bottles, and he carried pints and half pints of cream just in case a customer needed more. But my favorite recollection of Don Bockoven's milk route were the quart bottles of chocolate milk, made fresh each day in the Willow Tree Dairy milk cooler room.

As I got older, and took a summer job on the local road department, I always looked for Don's Divco milk truck, so I could flag him down and buy a quart of that terrific ice cold chocolate milk…what a treat!

On alternate years, Don and Frank Bockoven would plant corn in our back field, and that always resulted in the greatest hiding mazes a kid could create. When Don would drive up to cut the corn on his M with an International Harvester 2-row corn picker, we would rush out from the house again and help make the corn stalks into stacks. These always made great Indian teepees and forts to hide in. Cap pistols and a game of cowboys and Indians always followed the corn harvest in the Fall. It was my favorite time of the year!

Fall meant Halloween and carving pumpkins, and filling paper napkins with my Mother's flour to make flour bombs. Just the right weapon on a dark country road to turn any unsuspecting trick or treater into a powdery ghost! It was all harmless good natured fun, and no one ever took it too seriously or got bent out of shape by getting flour bombed. Of course toilet paper draped all the trees from our neighborhood all the way down into the center of town. The next day on the school bus, which Don's wife, Florence, drove, all of us kids could see first hand the toilet paper artistry we had created the night before!

Fall also meant glass gallon jugs of Lou Savage's homemade apple cider. Lou Savage lived up the hill from us, and had a big apple orchard. He also had a 1948 Farmall Cub that pulled a farm wagon around the orchard so he could collect the ripe apples and put them in wood bushel baskets. He also would let us neighborhood kids help pick the good apples off the ground and put them in the baskets.

This always meant a ride back from the orchard on the wagon to the cider barn where Lou made the most delicious hand pressed cider you ever tasted! He'd sell it to the neighbors, and anyone else who knew about this terrific Fall nectar for just a dollar a gallon ! My dad always kept a gallon jug of Lou's cider on our cold porch, and because it wasn't pasteurized, you needed to drink it within a week, or it would turn to apple cider vinegar.

Our next door neighbors had an apple orchard that Lou kept mowed with his Cub and a #22 sickle bar mower. I'd watch Lou on that Cub mowing around that orchard for what seemed like hours, through the split rail fence.

I guess these early memories have stayed fondly with me all these years. I never did become a farmer, instead I became a salesman like my dad, and worked as a radio announcer too, but I always promised myself that I'd get a Farmall tractor or two just for the fun of it. Today, I own, and have restored, a 1946 McCormick-Deering Farmall M, and a 1948 McCormick-Deering Farmall Cub with a #22 sickle bar mower. I show them at antique tractor and engine shows around the state and drive them around our country roads, just to charge up their batteries …and mine! Somehow, every time I'm on those tractors, I can travel back and visit those times and people who helped shape my life. They're GREAT recollections of a much simpler time in our history that won't ever come again. I'm convinced this is why so many people my age buy old tractors and antique cars and trucks…the time machines of our past!

A Farm Lad's Fantasy

BY ORLAN SKARE

Orlan Skare was raised on a farm near Bagley, Minnesota, in the 1930s, earning his love for tractors and farming firsthand. He went on to serve as a traveling salesman for six years for Big Red—the International Harvester Company. He later became a professor of marketing and sales at the Willmar, Minnesota, technical college.

After he retired, Skare began putting down on paper recollections of his farming youth as a way to pass them on to his children and future generations. He has written of myriad memories, from the pain and suffering imposed by old-fashioned cast-iron tractor seats to the window that was opened to the world when radio arrived on the farm. His essays have appeared in Willmar's *West Central Tribune*.

Skare composed this collection of recollections in honor of the Johnny Popper.

A farm lad operates a horse-drawn mower
Cutting a band of sweet-smelling hay
But he dreams of a time when horses are pastured
When power-farming offers a more promising way.

"Why buy gasoline for a tractor when you can raise oats and hay to fuel horses?" While Dad's reasoning made some sense in the cash-short early 1930s, it resulted in our farm being one of the last in the neighborhood to have a tractor.

The absence of a tractor on our farm only served to enhance my fascination for them. I had already decided that draft horses were sweaty, smelly, unpredictable beasts, interested in a young boy only if he was carrying a bucket of oats.

One of my early recollections is of a neighborhood thresherman turning into our farm driveway towing a threshing machine behind a steel-wheeled John Deere Model D. As he passed over a corner of Mom's well-tended garden to set his thresher between the round, tapered stacks of grain bundles, I recall thinking, "Mom's going to be angry about the rows of holes dug by the steel tractor cleats." I even tried to kick some of the clods of dirt back into the holes. Of course Mom wasn't angry; this was an acceptable reality of the times.

As the tractor operator was backing and turning his John Deere D to belt up to the thresher, I noticed him moving a long broomhandle-like lever back and forth. This didn't mean much to me at the time but I was later to learn that this was the infamous John Deere hand-clutch lever. The operator who had been standing while belting to the thresher had demonstrated a primary advantage of the hand clutch—its availability whether sitting or standing.

The John Deere D was considered a pretty big tractor at the time. I enjoyed watching the thresherman starting the engine. He first opened the petcock on each of the two, large cylinders in order to relieve some of the compression. After starting the engine by turning the large flywheel by hand, the engine made loud wheezing and spitting noises until the petcocks were closed.

Later in the 1930s, Dad and Mom gave serious thoughts to purchasing a small tractor that could be used both for haying and minor tillage work. International Harvester, Allis-Chalmers, and Ford-Ferguson had dealerships in Bagley. However, Dad and I favored the John Deere Model H, somewhat smaller than the more-popular Model B, but the closest John Deere dealer was in Fosston, Minnesota, twenty miles to the west of Bagley. How I dreamed about driving that little John Deere H!

But alas, we didn't act quickly enough and the outbreak of World War II killed our tractor-purchasing plans. We limped along during the wartime years with a "bug," a shortened Model A truck chassis that got us by quite well for haying, but was not very efficient for tillage purposes.

The two-cylinder design of early John Deere tractors provided a sound quite different from that of most other tractors. Wives of "Johnny Poppers" reportedly were able to determine when their husbands idled down the tractor for the trip home for lunch or dinner. This enabled them to have the food hot and on the table for the husband's arrival.

But there were other tractors with unique sounds. There were several Fordson tractors in our northern Minnesota neighborhood, and we could pinpoint their location a mile or two away by the transmission howl: "Sounds like Joe's working up his southwest forty this morning." Sometimes we could hear two or more Fordsons at the same time. Now bring in a farm dog with sensitivity to high-pitched sounds and you could have a howling country chorus!

The IHC Mogul and several other early tractors had one-cylinder engines that offered unique sounds of their own. These usually had heavy flywheels to smooth the engine's action, and many had governor-controlled intermittent firing and compression release. Someone claimed to be able to rapidly recite Abraham Lincoln's Gettysburg Address between the Mogul's firings while idling with no load. A dubious claim but the point is made.

Willmar, Minnesota, neighbor Irv Tallakson pointed out that the early Oliver 70 with six cylinders was especially smooth and quiet in operation, probably aided by the fact that Oliver was early in using full engine cowling.

The steam-traction engines like those made by J. I. Case and Aultman & Taylor offered a paradox of sound. In spite of their huge size, they made little engine noise. These powerful engines were often almost inaudible when belted to a noisy threshing machine.

Finally, as a youngster I learned that there was a perverse way to create a sequential medley of sounds when pitching grain bundles into a threshing machine. I accidentally tossed a bundle crossways into the feeder. The threshing machine groaned as the bundle entered the cylinder, the tractor snorted loudly as the governor signaled to recover engine speed, and the thresherman bounded up cursing "What the heck are you doing, boy?" Definitely not a mistake to repeat again the same day.

Before the end of World War II, I was drafted into the army, and upon discharge promptly entered college, got married, graduated, and began a job search. I still had tractor fantasies and my wife Beverly had some uncles who had fared well with International Harvester as company representatives. I brought a resume to the International Harvester district office, then just a few blocks east of the University of Minnesota campus that I had attended.

I began with IHC in March of 1950, worked for a short time in the office, before being transferred to a Wisconsin zone as a sales representative.

In the mid-1950s, a typical small Wisconsin town might have two or more full-line farm equipment dealers. IHC and John Deere were the most common, but Oliver, Case, Allis-Chalmers, Co-op, Ford, and others were also often represented.

As one part of my assistant zone manager assignment, I was to make farm calls with the dealer or a dealer's salesperson. The object was to get dealer personnel out to the farms, not simply waiting for customers to come through the front door.

These farm calls were fun and sometimes downright amusing. There was often lots of good-natured ribbing among John Deere and IHC owners. Long-time John Deere owner Don Caine of Willmar recently reminded me of a couple of "tit for tat" quips:

Question: Why are John Deere tractors painted green?

Answer: So they can hide in the grass when a Farmall comes by.

Question: Why are Farmall tractors painted red?

Answer: So when the parts fall off they can be easily spotted in the grass.

I recall an IHC dealer salesman telling me partly in jest that he was willing to call on most farmers but hesitant to call on a John Deere owner. He further explained that in his experience, John Deere owners were so tired of being referred to as "Johnny Poppers" that they became downright irrational when someone proposed the four-cylinder engine used by IHC.

I'm now in retirement after teaching marketing for twenty-six years at Willmar Technical College (now Ridgewater College). I'm in reasonably good health except for minor bouts of DLD (acronym for Divided Loyalties Dilemma). For example, as I poke around my garage, I still wonder if there isn't some way that I could squeeze my childhood love, a John Deere H—or maybe a Farmall B temptress—into one of the garage corners. Now wait: If I were to put a canvas cover over my trailered boat and put it outside, maybe I could have one of each! Dilemma resolved.

The "before" picture: Ray Baltes' Oliver Super 88 before he began the restoration journey.

The "after" picture: Ray Baltes' Oliver Super 88 ready to work again.

Super 88 Versus Not-So-Super Man

BY RAY BALTES

Ray Baltes grew up on a farm near Hampton, Iowa, but left after high school to pursue a career in journalism. He served as photo editor for the *Charles City* (Iowa) *Press*, then as editor of his hometown newspaper, the *Hampton Chronicle*. Deciding it was time to slow down, he left the newspaper business to spend more time with his family, write books, and help out on his dad's farm.

This essay is part of a book Baltes is at work on chronicling the legacy of his family's Oliver Super 88 tractors.

I grew up on a small farm in the northern part of Iowa in the 1960s and '70s, so from an early age I was fascinated with tractors. We always had a tractor on the farm, of course, but visiting my grandpa's farm was a special treat. My grandpa favored Oliver tractors, and at times had owned an Oliver 70, an 88 Row Crop, and a Super 88. I loved the soothing green color of these tractors, and the quiet purr of their motors.

Grandpa Baltes's Oliver Super 88 tractor held a special place in my heart. He would hoist me up onto his lap, shift the mighty machine into gear, and take me for rides down the long, grassy lane running along the field just east of the farmyard. I reveled in the characteristic whine of the big Oliver's gears as we bumped along. The smooth purr of the motor, along with the feeling of Grandpa's arms wrapping around me to reach the steering wheel, gave me a sense of security and happiness that I would never forget. As I rode, I would watch the tread of the giant rear tires passing in front of the fender. I could look to my left and see the field of very tall cane that was grown as cattle feed at that time. To my right was a narrow pasture and a ridgeline covered with massive stones removed from the farmland and piled high above the creek below. If it was fall and the harvest was complete, I might get the extra special experience of riding all the way around the 320-acre farm. I always wished those rides would never end.

Years later, I would relive those glorious trips down the lane, but not before my patience, my strength, my sanity, my body, and my family had been severely tested.

As I reached my 40s, I began longing to return to the farm way of life. I began spending more time at my folks' farm, helping out in any way I could. Chores that I once had despised, such as cleaning out the chicken house, mowing the yard, or discing the field, now became simple pleasures.

Then it happened.

One day, my dad came home with a 1954 Farmall Super H tractor. The old machine was in fairly rough shape, but after a great deal of cleaning, tinkering, repairing, and a shiny coat of paint applied by a local painter, it looked like brand new. I had hours of fun driving the antique machine around the farm and the surrounding gravel roads. A seed had been planted that would grow like the proverbial beanstalk.

Late one evening, I was surfing the Internet when I came across a website devoted to antique tractors. The site also featured photo ads of old tractors for sale, so I quickly dove in to see what I could find. I had no intention whatsoever of actually buying a tractor as I scrolled my way down the listings. Honest!

For the next month, I'd spend every available moment surfing through the old tractor ads, subconsciously hoping for that one deal of a lifetime tractor located somewhere in Iowa. Suddenly, there it was. "Oliver 88 with loader." What's more, the tractor was only about 40 minutes from my home. It sounded too good to be true. To this day, my family looks back on that moment as the time when Dad lost his mind.

The following evening I made the drive to the tiny town I had never heard of, and where the tractor was located. I noted with pleasure that the roads to the community were all very good, and would make the drive home an easy one.

I climbed on, turned on the switch, and pushed the starter button. Nothing. I tried again. Nothing. Since the seller was an auto mechanic and the tractor was sitting behind his shop, he simply wheeled out a booster cart and hooked it up. After a bit of cranking, the old girl finally fired, coughing up a good deal of smoke in the process. I didn't care the least bit.

Now, I wasn't about to buy an old tractor without taking it for a test drive. I remembered from my Grandpa's tractor that old Olivers had a two-range shift pattern: reverse one, first, second, and fifth gears were on the bottom half of the pattern; reverse two, third, fourth, and sixth gears were on the top. Figuring I'd start out slow, I shifted into second, revved the engine, and took off. I tried first gear, but I couldn't find it. Same with fifth gear. Low reverse worked fine, though. Then I tried the upper range of gears, starting with high reverse. It worked just fine. So did fourth. But when I tried third and sixth gears, I couldn't get the shifter to find the notch. In other words, only the left half of the shift pattern worked. I didn't care. After all, this was the Oliver of my dreams! I was sure the problem had to be minor. It would probably take me just a few minutes to fix.

The tires were very badly worn, and one rear tire had a slow air leak. The seller had to put air in that tire while I was there just so the tractor could be safely driven. One front tire was completely flat. It was also missing more than a few parts. So what? When you're looking at something you desperately want, you tend to forgive its little flaws and quirks.

My mind was made up: I was going to buy this tractor, take it home, and restore it to like-new condition. Never mind that I had never restored an old tractor, or that I had never even turned a wrench on an Oliver and knew nothing of their inner workings. I had, after all, taken many rides on my Grandpa's old Super 88, which made me uniquely qualified to undertake this project, right?

After about an hour of hemming and hawing, a price was agreed upon, hands were shaken, and I backed the flatbed trailer into place for loading my new prize.

Looking back, right then is when I should have jumped into my pickup and raced for home. But the thought never crossed my mind.

Once again, the tractor didn't want to start, so it was given a boost. I decided to back the tractor onto the trailer so it would be easier to get it off at my dad's farm. I worked the shifter into low reverse, and eased back towards the ramps. That's as far as the tractor would go. The old tires would just spin. I tried again, but the worn-out rubber refused to grip the steel ramps. Switching to plan B (as if there had been a Plan B), I backed the trailer up to a rise so that the tractor would have less of an incline to negotiate. No go, no matter how many times I tried. Finally, I backed the trailer up to a sharp slope at the side of a road, hoping to use the steep ground as a ramp to gain momentum. Sort of like Evel Knievel used when he jumped his motorcycle.

I shifted into high reverse, took a deep breath, gunned the engine, popped the clutch, and the tractor took off like the space shuttle! I hadn't anticipated the speed with which the old tractor would hit the trailer, and I was nearly thrown off of the spring-less seat! At the same time, I was scrambling to find the clutch and brake pedals so I wouldn't go careening into the back of my pickup! Somehow, I managed to regain control and bring the tractor to a halt just in the nick of time. I turned around to look over my shoulder, and instead of trailer, I saw only the bed of my pickup. I never once considered just how close to disaster I had come. Little did I know the worst was far from over.

I have a full-sized, two-wheel-drive pickup with a six-cylinder engine and a manual transmission. Although it had a heavy-duty trailer hitch, it did not have light or brake hookups for the trailer. By the time I had haggled down the price and gotten the tractor loaded and ready to go, the sun was beginning to set. I would have to drive home on the graveled back roads to avoid running into trouble with the law. I began to feel a little nervous.

My truck creaked and groaned as it struggled to pull away with the tractor-laden trailer, but it had no problem getting down the four or so miles of paved road before I had to hit the gravel. Maybe this wouldn't be so bad, after all. Or maybe it would…

The sun happened to set at precisely the same time I turned the rig onto the first of many miles of graveled roads. I turned my lights on, and quickly learned that the heavy trailer pushed down on the back of my truck so that my headlights were pointing skyward. As the evening grew blacker, so did my vision. Driving on unknown roads is always bit nerve-wracking, and doing it at night with while essentially blind-folded is enough to make most men cry. But the worst was yet to come.

I had also neglected to consider the fact that a relatively light, two-wheel-drive pickup would have a very difficult time stopping a 2,500-pound heavy equipment trailer loaded with a 5,000-pound tractor and 2,000-pound loader on gravel. After just a mile on the gravel road, I came to a T-intersection. Unfortunately for me, the intersection came at the end of a long downward slope. Thinking ahead, I applied the brakes early, but all they did was lock up! The truck and trailer continued its forward motion straight towards the deep ditch ahead as if it were a sled speeding down a snowy hill. I pondered screaming as I imagined my pickup being pushed straight down into the deep ditch, with the tractor crashing down right on top of me. I already knew my wife would be a bit angry when I showed up with a rusty old tractor; she would be madder than a wet hen if I came home flat! Thinking quickly, I decided a better course of action would be to let up on the brakes and try to slow the rig by downshifting. I shifted into a lower gear, gunned the engine, and gingerly let out the clutch. The wheels skidded a bit as they tried to find traction, and I breathed a huge sigh of relief when, just as I was ready to bail out the door, the tires grabbed and began to slow the rig down. The truck, trailer, and tractor came to a stop so close to the edge that as I looked over the hood of the pickup, all I could see was the cornfield on the other side of the ditch. I had to back up about 50 feet just so I could make the turn onto the next stretch of gravel. Whew!

With a valuable lesson learned, I went no higher than second gear during the rest of the trip, crawling along at a snail's pace. Working against me was the fact that none of the roads I took seemed to go more than a couple of miles before coming to another T-intersection. And, it seemed as if every one of those T-intersections was at the bottom of a steep hill. Because of this, what should have been a 45-mile trip stretched into something more like 140 miles. Or so it seemed as I inched along at about 20 miles per hour, straining through the blackness to see what cruel hazard awaited me up ahead. I don't remember the exact time I pulled into my dad's farm, but I'm pretty sure it was well past midnight, and I did it with another terrific sigh of relief. I pulled the trailer into the farmyard, turned off the truck, got out, and barely resisted the urge to kiss the ground. I felt almost like I had just successfully scaled Mt. Everest. With my eyes closed and one hand tied behind my back!

I was exhausted, but at the same time as giddy as a schoolboy. I owned a real tractor!

I arose early the next morning so I could get right to work on my tractor. Step one was to closely inspect the machine for the first time in the bright daylight. I began to see things I had missed the previous evening—before I had written out the check. Things that I probably should have seen as red flags. There were a lot of them.

My dad pointed out the first problem. A typical old farmer, he gets right to the point, and doesn't like horsing around.

"You know, it's got two different rear wheels," he said.

I hadn't noticed before, but he was right. One rear wheel was pressed steel, likely from an old Minneapolis-Moline tractor, and the other was cast iron, which was correct for the Oliver.

I also couldn't help but notice the radiator had a leak, and hydraulic fluid seeped from every seam in the hydraulic system. Both of the front wheels were missing at least one mounting bolt. The steel frame holding the seat had somehow been bent downward on its left side, making the seat tilt down on that side. The gearshift knob was missing. The front grill halves were so badly bent they wouldn't even come close to mounting on the tractor. A rusty old muffler from an old car sat perched over the exhaust manifold.

Before I saw more than I really wanted, I decided to hop onto the tractor and see if I couldn't get it fired up. The battery was completely dead, so I hooked it to a charger.

While the battery was charging, my dad and I managed to manhandle the tractor forward just enough to get the trailer ramps into place. This meant that I could now simply drive the old girl off, once the battery was charged.

Silly me.

Sure, the battery turned the starter, but as soon as the engine would sputter to life, it would promptly die.

Finally resorting to Plan B (which should have been to turn the truck and trailer around and head straight back to where the tractor came from), my dad got out his big International tractor, and we pulled the old Oliver off the trailer.

I then began the intricate process of figuring out why the old tractor wouldn't start.

Much of the next day, too, was spent on resuscitation efforts. The day after that, the same. My dad and I tried just about everything we could think of. We carefully removed each wire, one at a time, and tested it to see if it was good. We drained, cleaned, and refilled the gas tank, just in case bad fuel was the problem. We checked the starter and the ignition switch countless times. We even tried pulling the tractor to get it started, but even that failed.

"Did you check the gas?" my wife, Julie, would ask. "It sounds like it's out of gas."

"I've already checked it, and there's half a tank," I would answer.

Sheepishly admitting failure, I finally towed the thing under a shady tree and began the tedious process of removing parts for cleaning and restoration. My dad was looking the tractor over as I was removing the grill, and he suggested I might want to empty and clean the glass fuel filter reservoir.

"Make sure to close the fuel valve before you take it off," Dad cautioned.

I reached in and grabbed the valve.

"It's already closed," I said.

Silence.

We looked at each other. I have rarely felt more foolish. When the seller and I were cinching down the tractor, he had apparently turned off the fuel flow because it had a slight drip. He didn't tell me, and I never thought to check to make sure it was on. Like I said, I was no mechanic.

I opened the valve. I turned on the ignition switch and hit the button. The old tractor fired right up. Three days of nerve-racking struggles, and all I had needed to do was turn on the gas!

Before I shut the motor off, I made sure to give my young son, Tommy, an obligatory ride around the farmyard on the old Oliver. At that point, I had no idea when—or even if—he would get another chance to go for a spin with me.

Now, my stupidity only runs so deep. I knew the engine needed a little work, so I purchased the necessary shop manuals that would help me do it myself. All they did was show me that if I ever wanted to see this tractor run again, I had better leave the work to a trained mechanic.

Every few days I would drop by the repair shop to see how things were going. Each time, I found the tractor taken further apart, and with one or more freshly discovered problems.

It didn't take long before the "couple of repairs" I had hoped for turned into a long list of major work. It didn't take me long to figure out that the more often I stopped at the shop to check on the repairs, the more repairs I learned were needed. Unfortunately, staying away did little to reduce the amount of work required to repair the tired old tractor. By this time, I knew the repair bill was going to rival the Gross National Product, but I didn't mind. The tractor would soon be running like new.

Where I live, the highlight of the year is the county fair. Our fair is one of the best small fairs in the state, and draws visitors from across the country. It's the folksy, "Charlotte's Web" kind of county fair that is rarely seen today. Women from across the county bring in their best pies, vegetables, or fruits in the hopes of taking home a coveted blue ribbon, just like in Mayberry. Only the names are different. I can't recall an Aunt Bea or a Thelma Lou ever being on the list of winners.

One of the truly neat things about our fairgrounds is that it has a massive, free parking area in a hayfield just across the road from the main entrance. A number of years earlier, the fair board purchased covered shuttle wagons for hauling people from their cars to the gate. These trailers are pulled each year by antique tractors, and I had foolishly promised myself and Tommy that I would pull shuttles this year with a freshly restored Oliver 88.

When the tractor was finally ready to be taken home from the shop, there was less than a month until the start of the fair. I really needed about 12 months to complete all the work required to restore the old tractor, but I decided to plug onward towards my goal. I would simply start work earlier in the day, and wrap things up later in the evening. If my family wanted to see me, they knew where to find me.

Prior to restoring my old Oliver, my mechanical background consisted of tinkering with lawnmowers, completing minor repairs around the house, and the occasional repair of small items. I had never before worked on a tractor, but how different could it be? It was simply a matter of scale. A lawn mower used gas and oil. So did a tractor. A lawnmower had a sparkplug that caused a spark that ignited gas fumes, causing a cylinder to move. Same with a tractor. I could fix a lawnmower with a screwdriver and a couple of wrenches. Not so with a tractor.

I figured the best way to learn how the old Oliver worked was to simply take it apart. I would have to dismantle it eventually for painting, so with socket set in hand, I went to work.

I didn't take long for me to realize I was in way over my head. In fact, it only took about three bolts. Admitting defeat would have been too unmanly to bear, so I plugged along, trying desperately to remember the place for each bolt as I removed it from the tractor. I even had a clever system for helping me to remember where the bolts went. I used cans to hold bolts from each part: one can would hold the radiator mounting bolts; another would hold the gas tank mounting bolts; and so on. It was only later that I realized I had forgotten to label each can so I would know where its bolts went.

It was time to paint. This was my baby, so I had determined right from the beginning that I would do everything the right way, regardless of difficulty, time or cost. Okay, not cost, but I did want the final product to be one I could be proud of.

One by one, each piece of sheet metal from the tractor was taken to my backyard, where it was sanded, hammered into shape, and polished. This was done primarily using wire brushes and an electric drill. Well, actually I went through three electric drills and about two dozen brushes before the job was done. I also learned that wire brushes, when used on electric drills, can be dangerous weapons. Those tiny little wire bristles tend to come loose, and fly like an arrow to the nearest thing. I now know what a porcupine feels like, and even days after a sanding session I would find those little wires in my socks, shirt, and even my shorts!

While the large, flat pieces could be fairly easily stripped and prepped using power tools, there were still hundreds of corners, curves, cups, holes, and other odd shapes that required hand sanding and polishing. This was the really hard work, and required the use of steel wool, sandpaper, files of different shapes and sizes, and lots of elbow grease. At first,

I had tried using paint stripper, but all that did was make a huge, smelly mess. I would have to do it by hand. Each night I would find myself barely able to lift a glass of water to my mouth because my hands and arms were so tired. My son would giggle at me as I grunted and struggled to hoist anything heavier than a cookie.

After spending what seemed like 17,000 hours prepping the tractor, now I could begin the fun part: painting.

Mistake number one was attempting to paint my tractor outdoors. Mistake number two was choosing to paint my tractor outdoors in the heat of summer. Mistake number three was waiting until evening to paint so that I would not be working in the hottest part of the day. Mistake number four was even thinking I could come close to a professional-looking paint job by doing it myself.

Summer evenings in Iowa mean one thing: bugs. Millions of them. At times they are so thick that they look like small clouds drifting across the farmyard. They range in size from huge June bugs that sound like helicopters passing overhead, to what we call "no-see-ums," tiny little black bugs that bite like the devil.

Every one of them had the same mission: get stuck in my paint.

I would take great care to adjust the paint sprayer so that I was putting on the perfect coat. I worked slowly, being careful to avoid runs or thin spots. Each evening I painted a few parts. One evening it was the wheels. Another, it was the fenders and sheet metal.

The trouble was, each morning, when I'd inspect the previous night's work, I'd find thousands of bugs stuck in my masterpiece. Some could be carefully removed with a tweezers without leaving much of a mark. The vast majority would leave a sickening hole in the paint when pulled off.

Each day, then, I would have to strip all the paint off of most of the parts I had painted the previous evening, carefully sand them down to the primer, then paint them again. After a several days of this, I decided to skip removing all the paint and simply sand the surface around the bug spot smooth, then paint that only that area again. This meant that different areas of a particular part might be painted over the course of several different evenings, with different wind conditions, temperatures, and humidity. You know that kind of velvety look that soybean leaves get when the wind blows them like waves on water? That's sort of how my paint job looked. Actually, I think the cheap quality paint I was using actually helped at this point. The overall finish was dull enough that many imperfections were difficult to see unless the light was just right.

All of this went on the week before the start of our county fair, so time was quickly ticking away. I was forced to take a shortcut here and there that I shouldn't have, but I was determined to have the tractor ready for pulling those shuttle wagons at the fair.

Opening day of the fair found me starting the intricate process of putting the tractor back together. I had no way of knowing if I would be able to get everything back in the right place, and I suspected my family had a pool going on the question.

The temperature rose well above 90 degrees as I reassembled the tractor bolt by bolt. This is when I discovered I had forgotten to label my bolt cans. I had a large jug of cold water with me, but not even that was able to cool me down. I worked very carefully; I sure didn't want to put another big scratch in the paint now! By some miraculous stroke of luck, everything found its way back into the right place, and by late in the afternoon the old girl was together once more. I don't know if I got every bolt in the right place, but I managed to find a place for each one, and there were none left over.

That night I fell right to sleep, knowing that the following day would mark the public unveiling of the Super 88. As I slept, I had dreamt of a star-studded Hollywood-style premier, complete with paparazzi and lights searching the sky.

Lots of folks around the county had been following my restoration progress through a series of columns I had written as editor of the local newspaper. I often wonder just how much wagered money changed hands when I proudly drove my Super 88 through the fairgrounds gate. The first person I saw as I drove in was Wendell Miller, the mechanic who had brought my old tractor back to life. He was pulling a shuttle wagon with his own antique tractor, a Massey Harris 33, and when he gave me a "thumbs up," I couldn't have been happier.

The paint on the tractor was not even completely dry, and there were no stickers or nameplates to make the tractor complete, but that didn't matter. For the next four hours, I found myself accepting countless handshakes, "thumbs-up," congratulations, and words of encouragement from just about everybody who set foot on my shuttle. The old girl purred like a kitten as she tugged the shuttle behind, and I didn't even notice the extreme heat or dust. I was also glad I had put a padded, adjustable-suspension seat on the Oliver. Or at least my backside was.

Alas, the end of my shift came far too quickly, and I had to drive the old girl back to my house before it got dark because I had not yet installed the lights. That night, the loud whine of the rear end was barely noticeable as I sped down the highway towards home. I was too busy basking in my glory.

The next several months were spent completing the restoration. Decals were applied, and a rearview mirror and a cup holder were mounted on the dash. With the fair over, I could take my time, and for once, I actually found myself having fun working on the Oliver. That didn't mean the work was easy—or painless. The tractor caught fire not once, but three times (hey, I'm not an electrician, either), I broke two ribs when I tripped and fell on a steel tool box, I suffered second degree burns on my backside when I fell asleep on a heating pad after straining my low back, and I nearly lost the tip of a finger while foolishly trying to bend part of the fan shroud while the engine was running.

It had been a very trying spring and summer, but all of the hard work, blood, sweat, and tears finally paid off that fall.

On a gorgeous, golden autumn day, I decided I'd take Ollie for her first real ride through the countryside. I gassed her up, and off I went down gravel roads, with no particular destination in mind. After about an hour on the road, I realized that I was only a couple of miles from my grandpa's old farm. Had I unconsciously pointed the Oliver towards its destiny, or had Ollie somehow led me there? I steered the old Oliver in that direction. It was time for the main event.

My excitement began to grow as I drove the Super 88 into the farmyard and past the numerous buildings and sheds. There it was ahead of me: the very lane on which my grandpa used to give me rides with his Oliver Super 88. I stopped the tractor for a moment, thinking back to those happy days so long ago. I set the brake and climbed off so I could savor the moment. I felt like a kid again.

I could stand it no more. I climbed back on, shifted the tractor into fourth gear, which was my best guess as to what gear my grandpa had used, and let out the clutch.

It was perfect. Here I was, on the same kind of tractor, on the very same lane. Forty years disappeared in a heartbeat. The lane was exactly as it was back then, and the purr of the engine and hum of the gears were precisely as I remembered them. All the trials and tribulations I had endured until now suddenly did not matter. My dream had finally come true. I drove all the way down the bumpy lane, savoring every inch. The tall cane had long since been replaced by corn, but the pasture and ridge overlooking the creek below were unchanged. Not all of the corn had been harvested yet, so I wasn't able to drive around the full 320 acres. That didn't matter one bit. I felt a special sense of satisfaction, of achievement. I had fulfilled the promise I made to myself so many years ago.

As I turned the tractor back towards my dad's farm, I cast one more look back at the old lane. Somehow, I just knew that Grandpa Baltes had been with me on that ride, and the smile on his face and joy in his heart were as big as mine.

Grandpa Baltes cuts hay back in the day with the family's Oliver Super 88.

Sixty Years With a
John Deere Model D

BY BIRD J. VINCENT

Bird J. Vincent lives on a centennial farm in Freeland, Michigan. He has written numerous articles chronicling life on his farm, from the old threshing days to memories of his favorite tried-and-true farm machines.

This article is a sort of timeline history of his family's John Deere Model D, chronicling every repair and modification made to the machine over the years as well as the nostalgic memories those simple repairs bring back.

O ur 1938 John Deere Model D, serial number 134761, was delivered in the spring of 1939. I was only five years old, but I can still remember the truck and trailer pulling into the driveway. The D had rubber front tires and steel lugs, and cost about $1,300.

That shiny new tractor was a great embarrassment to my late father a few days after it arrived. For some reason which even Mr. Thinker can't figure out, it was made with small, high-speed industrial sprockets on the drive axle. A neighbor, now in his late eighties, lived at the second farm north. He had an outbuilding on skids and wanted it moved. Dad went up with his big new D and hooked on to it. He couldn't move it. Another neighbor came and moved the building with an old Avery.

After Dad drove home, it didn't take him long to get to the hand crank on the phone and ring up the dealer to come and fix the D. The dealer fixed the tractor on the wooden platform of a hay wagon scale we had in our front yard at that time. The transmission hasn't been worked on since except to change the gear oil.

The first tractor on our farm was a 1918 International Titan. I have pictures of it and a receipt for $1,557 dated November 8, 1918; the receipt includes the tractor and a John Deere three-bottom plow. The next tractor was an International 15/30. Then came the John Deere D, followed by a Ford 9N, Deere H, Deere A, Deere 3010, 4020, and 4250, and my son's Minneapolis-Moline ZB and Deere B pulling tractors.

Dad made a wooden toolbox that sits on the left side of the platform in front of the radiator shutter lever. It is painted International red. I spent many hours sitting on that toolbox when I was small. One time, Dad was plowing and I looked down and saw the flywheel wobble. It was ready to come off. Dad stalled the D and fixed the problem. The flywheel still runs one-eighth inch beyond the crankshaft, but hasn't come loose in years.

When I was a little older, I would sit on the D as it powered the Case twenty-eight-inch thresher, Keck Gonnerman beaner, or Papec silo filler. I could operate the clutch and throttle when Dad would signal me by hand—a twirling hand above his head to speed up, hand up and down to slow, hand across the throat to stop. My four older brothers had to help with the heavy work like pitching bundles or carrying grain bags. Later, the two oldest went into the Army during World War II.

Dad threshed for about ten neighbors during the 1940s. When moving from farm to farm, he would drive the D and pull the thresher and one wagon. I would drive the 1941 Ford 9N, pulling two more wagons. My older brothers would drive the 1939 Mercury. Dad had canvas to cover the thresher, loaded wagons, and D at night. We carried planks to put down when we crossed the one tarvie road in the neighborhood.

I can still remember when I grew enough to be able to pull the flywheel and start the D. But it started hard when it was warm, so many times we would let it idle at meal times and only stop it to refuel.

It is still fun to watch a boy try to start it. You have to be strong enough to turn the flywheel and smart enough to let go when it fires. The sound of it starting is so pleasant that I look forward to it each spring and have even tape-recorded that sound for posterity.

Standard Oil made a special fuel for the John Deeres called "Power Fuel." When Standard stopped supplying Power Fuel, Dad put in a two-compartment overhead tank, with gasoline in one end and No. 1 fuel oil in the other. He would put both nozzles in the main tank and hold both open at the same time. It would start on gas, then switch and run on the blend. But you had to be sure the carburetor ran empty when it was shut down because it wouldn't start on the blended fuel.

We pulled an eight-foot double disc that would load up and be difficult to turn in sandy ground. Sometimes I had to unhook, back in on an angle, and hook up with a log chain we always had on the tractor. When the disc was turned sharp, it would unload. You would have to get it turned around and then rehook to the drawbar.

We still have the John Deere twelve-foot springtooth drag that was hooked from drawbar to the evener with a V-chain. One time, I turned too short, the chain caught the back tire, and came up and dented the fender before I could stop.

I used the D and drag last spring to incorporate one-third acre of oats for our threshing bee. I spread the oats with a Cyclone spreader on the Ford 9N. It's easier than getting the FBB drill out and I like to have the D the first tractor working ground in the neighborhood each spring to show all the modern tractors the way.

The township had an Adams pull-type grader, the kind with the large hand wheels to set the depth at each end of the blade. I was driving and Dad was operating the grader, making a ditch. With every pass, the D was on more of a slant. Finally, it started to pound. Apparently it wasn't picking up oil. We decided the ditch was deep enough. (Mr. Thinker: Is the oil pickup off to one side?)

A dragline cleaned a large ditch on the south side of our farm and left the spoil in the field. To start to level it, we hooked up to a long barn beam with the D on one end and a neighbor's John Deere A on the other. The A was next to the ditch and would run a little ahead to give a grading action. But if the beam caught on a pile of dirt in the middle, I could keep moving and pull the A backward.

In 1947, the steel wheels were replaced with rubber tires. The man from the Firestone dealer came out and measured, took the wheels, cut the flat spokes off, and welded on thirty-inch rims and 15.5x30 tires (now 18.4x30). But he had measured wrong and they would not fit under the fenders. He tried to get Dad to take the fenders off, but Dad refused. So the Firestone dealer cut the spokes again and installed twenty-eight-inch rims and the closed-tread Firestone tires loaded with CaC12 solution. The tire man lost his job because of the mistake.

The left rim split on the inside in about 1965. The tire rubbed and was ruined. I had a new rim welded on and replaced the tire with a Gates open-tread tire. The ends of the Gates tread bars would rub the flywheel when the D was turned and the tire flexed. You could smell the hot rubber. The flywheel wore a groove in the tire.

In 1995, we welded a patch on one rim, sandblasted and painted the rims, and tried to install a new set of 18.4x28 Firestone tires. Again they were too large and rubbed. We put the old tires back on until we could get a set of 16.9x28 tires. We did not load these with CaC12. This tire man did not lose his job because we knew it would be close, but I wanted the larger size if possible.

We also replaced the front tires with 7.50x18 Goodyear five-rib, like the ones that came on it. The pulley side had been replaced because it was cut so badly by the thresher drive belt. But the flywheel side was the original 1938 tire. It was weathered some on the outside, but the inside looked great yet.

One time a fan blade broke off in the field and was never found. Another time, the D had a magneto problem while threshing navy beans on our farm. We ran the Keck Gonnerman beaner with a neighbor's Farmall M that day.

The D's engine was first overhauled at Rogers John Deere in LaPorte, Michigan. I can remember seeing it with the head off and seeing how large the piston bore was. My older brother, Jim, can remember the bill for a simple ring and valve grind was $45.

The next—and last—overhaul was done at Dad's brother's Ford dealership in Auburn, Michigan. This time, the block was removed and bored oversize. At the same time, a large Fram oil filter was installed just behind the gas tank. Fram no longer makes a replacement filter so it hasn't been changed for about thirty years. It still gets warm, so oil must flow through it.

We kept a spare magneto on hand for the D. It does not have the original on it now. A few years ago, we had the magneto and carburetor rebuilt. It runs great yet.

The steering got loose and we rebuilt it. A local machine shop made a new pin and bushing for where the wishbone attaches to the crankcase. We found out the hard way that the engine oil drains when you remove that pin. The crank arm at the bottom of the vertical steering shaft is welded to the shaft because the tapered splines are worn. This was a problem over the years. The tie rod ends and the bolts that hold the steering gear box were tightened. The steering is good now.

The D was stripped, primed, and painted in 1985. The hood is rusted near the radiator from water sloshing out and the top of the exhaust pipe has eroded away.

A few years ago, we found and purchased the same Co-op plow that the D used to pull. It had been sold twice. The third bottom has been removed, but two fourteens are enough to bring back the memories and my son can also pull it with his Deere B.

We have a threshing bee on our centennial farm every year, and operate the binders, threshers, and the silo filler with that old D. The fourth generation is now operating the D, and it should last for a good many more years to come.

Sis operates the hay binder.

Subterfuge

BY PATRICIA PENTON LEIMBACH

Patricia Penton Leimbach is farming's Erma Bombeck. Like Bombeck, author of numerous essays and books on being a housewife, Leimbach is a sage philosopher on the trials and tribulations of everyday life. She writes with a sharp pen about the joys and troubles, the hard work and humor, the meaning and value of rural living.

Leimbach was raised on a fruit farm near Lorain, Ohio. Alongside her now-late husband, Paul, a fourth-generation farmer, she has run End o' Way farm in Vermilion, Ohio, for more than four decades. But it is through her writing that Leimbach has become one of the best-known farm women in North America. For many years, she authored the weekly "Country Wife" column in the Elyria, Ohio, *Chronicle Telegram* newspaper. Leimbach also has three books to her credit, *A Thread of Blue Denim*, *All My Meadows*, and *Harvest of Bittersweet*, all filled with wit and wisdom culled from her firsthand farming knowledge concerning everything from raising puppies to driving farm tractors.

In this essay from *Harvest of Bittersweet*, she describes the brilliant subterfuge used by her husband to get her to agree that it is time for yet another new tractor on the farm.

Y ou can "smell" a new tractor coming two or three years ahead. The first thing a wife notices is that the thrill—of the old tractor, that is—is gone. He no longer fondles the fenders, caresses the hood. No more does he run in the face of a storm to get 'er under cover. A crumpled muffler may leap into the wind for months on end. The vinyl seat splits and he seems not to notice. Foam oozes from the rupture and is carelessly obscured beneath a feed bag. Gone is the pride that once moved him to slyly detour visitors through the tractor shed. It doesn't seem very important anymore who drives the old thing—the wife even gets a crack at it.

"Give you any trouble?" he'll ask casually at lunch. Then, as he chomps down on a cob of corn, he'll move into phase two of the buildup: innuendo and suggestion.

"Been startin' a little hard lately. Thought maybe you'd notice. . . . Shifts a little rough, don't you think?" You can agree or disagree. The psychological workup is in progress. The seeds of disturbances have been sown.

"D'ja notice how much oil that tractor's been burning?" he'll say to his son one day, making sure you're within earshot. Then early some morning he'll interrupt the bookkeeping by walking into the kitchen (ostensibly for something to eat) and remarking, "Guess how much we spent for repairs on the 706 last year?" And then he'll name a figure half again as high as the household budget.

"What?" you shriek. "On that new tractor?"

"That new tractor is ten years old."

"You're kidding."

"I am not kidding. We bought it the year the willow tree fell on the outhouse. Remember? I'll tell you how long we've had that tractor. We've had it so long it's paid for."

The next thing you know, there's a tractor dealer coming by on trumped-up charges, hanging around the gas pump, leaving slick, four-color brochures in your kitchen, "giving" your husband the kind of time he's charging $10 an hour for back at the shop.

Someplace in the campaign you'll be treated to the "poor lil' ol' me" routine.

"Russ and Chuck traded their John Deeres in on a coupl'a 4-wheel-drive Cases two years ago. Don, Lenny, George, and Bob—they've all had a complete tractor turnover since we bought that 706. . . ."

Then there's the scare technique: "Parts are gettin' harder and harder to locate for that machine. Wouldn't surprise me a bit if they quit making them altogether."

About this time you'll find a list of figures on a scratch pad conveniently placed to catch your eye—over the sink next to the telephone, on the back of the john. You think at first it's an inventory of all your holdings.

"Is this anything you want to keep?" you ask.

"Oh, that—that's just something the tractor dealer jotted down for me. Uhhh . . . some figures on a tractor—and a plow. New tractor takes a new plow. Says he'll take my old tractor on trade and give me just what I paid for it ten years ago. That takes 'er down to about fourteen thousand."

"Fourteen thousand dollars! Holy cow! We don't want to buy the business. We just need a tractor!"

You suddenly realize that it's all over.

My First—and Second—
Tractor

BY BLAKE FOHL WITH JOHN DIETZ

Blake Fohl has a classic story to tell. He was raised in a city but fell in love with farming while at college in Tennessee. He also liked marketing. For a while he rented a small farm while working at a retail farm store. Leaving that, after learning to farm, he went into the Tractor Supply Company. He emerged seventeen years later, in 2008, after serving as senior VP of marketing and advertising. He had married late, had a son, and discovered his boy liked riding with Dad in the tractor. He's quit the executive life and gone into full-time farming!

I was on the executive path for many years, and traveled quite extensively for 10 years, but finally got married and became a father for the first time when I was 45 years old. Our son, Zephan, was born in 2004. He is 5 now, and an important part of why I left Tractor Supply in May 2008.

Today our family has 500 acres of picturesque rolling land outside of metro Nashville, in middle Tennessee. But let me tell you about my first tractor, and my second tractor.

FIRST TRACTOR

I actually grew up in Nashville, but I went to a college prep school in Franklin, Tennessee. The majority of the students were from farm families, so I spent a lot of time in summer working on farms with them, putting up hay, helping seed, things like that. I developed a real affinity for the farm life, and the kind of people who were doing farming.

When I graduated from high school, and went to college, at first I was going to get a degree in marketing. Then I decided to change it to a degree in ag business. So I entered into the agricultural industry with the goal that, at some time, I would be able to farm, too.

I received a degree in agriculture from Tennessee Tech. I began working in the field of agriculture first with Southern States Cooperatives, out of Richland, Virginia, managing farmer co-ops. I left to work with Deville's as a dairy specialist. My next career was with a wholesale seed company, called Grain Seed. I managed the wholesale distribution points for them.

My first tractor was a little four-cylinder two-wheel-drive Massey Ferguson 165. It was primarily for bush-hogging and cutting feed. At the time, I was living in Kentucky and working for Purina Mills. I had rented about 120 acres of rolling grassland south of Louisville. It was just a rolling rough old cow farm, where I could fence off paddocks and produce enough hay to take care of 30 beef cows. There was probably 60 or 70 acres in pasture, probably 30 acres in hay and about 20 acres in woods and gullies and stuff that wasn't worth much. I grew a lot of sorghum-sudan and round-baled it for winter feed. I was there for about three years, in the mid-1980s.

That first tractor was like anything else, all about what you could afford. I tried to get as much horsepower as I could. The equipment was just a mish-mash. There was an old New Holland round baler. I don't remember the hay cutter or the brush cutter model. I'd go to an auction and buy something that looked like it would help get the job done, for as long as possible.

That tractor had the typical things you have with an old tractor. The tires didn't have enough tread. It used about as much oil as it did gas. It wasn't what you'd call a real smooth ride. There were no creature comforts, at all. To learn what all the levers and things did, I pretty much had to find someone who'd had one before because there was no labels, no stickers, left on it. It was a pretty rough old tractor, but it did what I needed and it served me well for what I could afford at the time. There's no comparison to it, now, at all.

I worked at the farm on evenings and weekends. During hay-time, you spent quite a bit of time at it. You had to go rake and cut and tie and bale. It was really harder on my butt than on my back. That seat wasn't very good. The original padding had all been rotted off. It just had a low pad you set on the seat and tied on with some string. There was a little back rest, but no arm rests. You weren't resting arms much, anyway. I had both hands on the steering wheel most of the time.

When you're working daytime for a company, a lot of farm stuff is done late at night. Many work nights ended at 9 or 10 o'clock. The hardest job I had with that tractor was keeping the lights working. I'd be in the middle of a big field, working at night, and the lights would go out. It would be the longest walk back to the barn to get the truck to get the tools to get the lights going again. I learned to carry along a flashlight, maybe after the second or third time.

Farming was something that, the more I did it, the more I wanted to do it but I was in that awkward place, too small to be big and too big to be small. The economics didn't work, so that I could stop doing what I was doing; so, I decided to work real hard at what I was doing so I could eventually do what I wanted to do.

That particular farming enterprise ended when I took a job with another company. I sold all the equipment and moved to a different part of the country. I was not back involved with farming until about 5 years ago, when I bought this farm.

SECOND TRACTOR

My last public job was with Tractor Supply Company. I began with them as a buyer in 1986 and worked my way up over the next 17 years. At the end, I was senior vice president of marketing and advertising. During my tenure, we went from having 149 stores doing less than $200 million in sales to having 800 stores doing almost $3 billion in sales.

Tractor Supply also transitioned, while I was there, from a regional store that focused on the full-time production farmer to a retail company focused on the needs of people living and wanting to live the rural lifestyle, more aspirationally than economically.

My experience in farming, being around farm people, and understanding their mindset really helped me on the marketing side to develop the brand and the communications setup to be able to talk to those people.

One of my projects, *Out Here* magazine, became a very aspirational magazine. It is hard to even see Tractor Supply in its own magazine. It's just about people living out here. During its inception, in the first couple years I was involved, we wanted to keep it very pure, very simple. It was really a brand connector for us. We hoped to see people coming in quarterly, picking it up, taking it home to be read by multiple people and passed along. Readers would think, "Tractor Supply must understand us."

We wanted our customers to understand that we knew about them, that we understood their lifestyle and we were actively seeking them out to learn more about them, to hear about them, and make good compelling reading at the same time.

While Tractor Supply was in a very public transition, Carrie and I were in a very private transition. It happened gradually, but today we actually own two private farm-based enterprises. At Hillview Farms LLC, I raise all-natural beef for high-end chef-owned-and-operated restaurants in the middle-Tennessee area, and sell freezer-beef to health-conscious people who are looking for all-natural products. Carrie operates Hillview Kennels on 11 acres. It is considered the ultimate location for breeding the highest quality German Shepherd dogs.

We own a couple of small farms and rent a couple, splitting them up with generous amounts of pasture space and feed production. We grow all our feed stock—corn, wheat, and a lot of hay. The hay is a mixture of alfalfa, orchard grass, timothy, and fescue, mostly.

Instead of a heavy airport travel schedule, I spend a lot of time moving equipment from one farm to another. When I began putting together the farm for this back-half journey of mine, I settled on New Holland equipment. I was finally able to get to the point that I could buy a new tractor. Until then, the tractors I'd bought and owned were older, used tractors, all different colors, affordable at the time.

My main tractor now is a New Holland TL100A four-wheel-drive tractor with a cab and air conditioning, and about 98 PTO horsepower. It offers a lot of visibility, and it's a very, very comfortable tractor. We're coming up to just over 2,000 hours on the meter now. I also have a New Holland TC48D, a four-wheel-drive 40-horsepower tractor that we call the barn tractor. We use it for everything. It's got a front-end loader; it's a handy little thing to have around.

The TL100A tractor is very stable and feels very comfortable on hillsides. I put fluid in the tires and run some big equipment with it. When you're bush-hogging with a 13-foot batwing mower on some of these hillsides, it's very stable and feels very safe. Then, when I get onto flat ground and put on the four-wheel-drive, it handles a 15-foot disc as well as tractors that have more horsepower.

FARMING LIFE

Having a little boy, wanting him raised in the country, understanding the farm life and all the things that go with it—the values, the ethics, understanding what work is all about, seeing things grow, understanding the cycle of life of plants and animals—I put together a plan to leave the corporate world and to become a full-time farmer.

For a while, I did both farming and marketing. I was in the tractor every evening, pretty much all weekend and all the vacation days and holidays. I really enjoyed the time I spent in the tractor and would kind of follow the hour-meter. About the time I bought my first new tractor, Zephan was getting to the age where he could ride inside the tractor cab with me. I was really amazed at the number of hours he could sit there in just total rapt attention. It didn't seem to matter whether we were discing, plowing, bush-hogging, planting corn, cutting hay, or baling hay.

I came to realize that the hour-meter was really sort of a meter on my passion. I thought about the number of hours I was working with a public company. While they were a great organization and providing me a lot of opportunity, it didn't take long to figure out that I really enjoyed the time I spent in the tractor and with my son a whole lot more than I did sitting in meetings, running from one airport to the next, catching one plane after another.

It really helped solidify the decision for me that what I really needed to do was go ahead, make the commitment to begin this other enterprise and to begin to move away from corporate life. Instead of living in business clothes, live in blue jeans, spend my time out in the fresh air, spend my time working on repairing equipment. It was an interesting transition, and I really look at that New Holland tractor hour-meter as being the indicator of not only the time I was spending in the tractor but the indicator of where my real passions lay.

I have spent pretty much my whole life serving farmers, always respecting them, getting to know an enormous number of them. One day I wanted to be able to do life as a farmer, but I was on another career path. As with a lot of careers, you get on a path and tend to stay in that path. It was a pretty big decision, leaving the executive business world to go out on your own. I could have stayed much longer, but then I would have been so tired and worn out that I wouldn't want to farm!

Lightning Strike

BY RANDY LEFFINGWELL

Photographer and writer Randy Leffingwell has become known and respected around the globe for his detailed chronicles of farm tractors and his eloquent photographs of old machinery that speak volumes about their stories. He is the author of numerous books, including *The American Farm Tractor*, *John Deere Farm Tractors*, *Caterpillar*, *Classic Farm Tractors*, *Farm Tractors: A Living History*, and more.

During his travels across North America while compiling his first tractor book, Randy met retired Denison, Iowa, farmer Ray Pollock and his 1939 McCormick-Deering Farmall F-20. Both Pollock and the Farmall had a story to tell about the end of horse farming and the dawn of the age of tractors.

"I've never in my life bought a new tractor, never even owned one close to new," Ray Pollock says with a touch of finality. After more than a half century of faming in Western Iowa, Pollock has retired, so the likelihood of his buying something new now is remote.

"I bought that F-20 there in 1948. It was a 1939 model and all I ever did to it was grind the valves about ten years ago. You don't need all this high-priced stuff. There's no advantage. These young people starting out haven't got a clue."

Pollock was born in 1915, the third of six children. When he was barely fourteen, the stock market crashed in New York City in October 1929. It was another three years, until Ray was seventeen, before the real depths of the Great Depression hit western Iowa. He was old enough to understand what was happening around him, to his family and their friends.

"Times were tough. Things were real bad. Nobody had anything: no money, no food. Hogs sold for three cents a pound, corn was a dime a bushel. A farmer could rent a farm for, say, ten dollars an acre. Didn't cost much more than that to buy. Except there was no money. City folks couldn't buy the food and farmers couldn't pay their rents or mortgages. You farmed what you had with what you had. There was no way we could go out and buy anything, let alone a tractor."

Pollock, his parents, brothers, and sisters survived the hard times, but the clarity of their memories colored their view of the future. Pollock learned the lessons of careful spending, of husbanding resources against the next hard time.

"I farmed with horses. That F-20 tractor was quite an improvement, you know. You gotta understand, with horses, everything takes time. By the time you harness up your five horses, well, it takes quite a while. You gotta let them rest at the end of each row. And then you gotta bring them in at noon, unhitch 'em, feed 'em, and get 'em watered. Then you can eat. Then back out, and work 'til near dark and when you come in, it's the same old thing over again. Day after day. It's really quite a bit of work. We did ten, sometimes twelve, acres in a day. Really moving. That's including the time to come in for dinner and going back out midday.

"Of course, I always had outlaws, too. Real jugheads. I didn't have good horses, well-trained ones. Couldn't afford them. Mine would as soon kick your head in or run away as work for you."

Keeping horses was work, too. They ate up as much as a fifth of Pollock's crop. They needed shoes and care. Their tack required attention. Even then, things happened that no one could foresee, that no one could control.

"In one single day, I lost three of those horses to lightning. Right out there in the field. No time to unhitch and get 'em to cover, to the barn. I was plowing and planting. And now I was down to just two horses. That's the only reason I even bought that tractor. I wasn't in any hurry to get one. I just had to get my seed into the ground.

"That Farmall was the first tractor I ever bought. But it made quite a difference, I'll tell you. With the hired man, with the F-20, we plowed all eighty acres in just four days, pulling two sixteen-inch plows. And harrowed it. All of that in just four days. That's maybe two weeks with the horses."

For the next forty-eight years, with time out only for the valve job, that tractor and Ray Pollock operated the farm every day. In 1995, shortly before his eightieth birthday, Ray's son, Bob, finally got him to retire. Bob, a scrap-metal dealer, spirited his father's old Farmall away, but not to the boneyards.

On Ray's birthday, Bob, who is also an antique tractor collector, presented his father with the F-20, completely restored.

Duck Soup

BY BILL VOSSLER

Bill Vossler deserves the title "tractor detective" for his extraordinary book, *Orphan Tractors*. His sleuthing to uncover the history of the lost tractor makes—from Avery to Rumely, Happy Farmer to Waterloo Boy—makes for a masterful collection of tractor lore. Bill is also a historian of toy tractors and regularly writes for *Toy Farmer* magazine.

In this story, Bill tells of a harrowing incident in his youth, when he learned to drive tractor, outran a prairie storm, and learned a bit more about himself as a person.

During summers on the North Dakota prairie, we were often forewarned of bad weather because we could see it pile up far off on the horizon through wavy sheets of heat, sometimes early in the day. And so most farmers in those days kept one eye cocked toward the horizon with a mind as to what the weather might allow them to do—or not to do—that workday.

But Gordie, the farmer I worked for, was no ordinary farmer. He owned a gift of gab, as well as the local sales barn (which, rumor had it, he had won in a high-stakes poker game in the back room of a local bar), and farming wasn't his highest priority. This was why he needed a hired hand, and eventually I filled that bill between my junior and senior years of high school after I had just turned seventeen.

Unfortunately, I was no normal hired hand. I knew as much about agriculture as you might expect from a farming-area city kid who had picked rock, hauled bales, and once or twice butchered chickens and pigs. This might not have been a problem, except that Gordie was seldom around to help me or direct me or give me advice.

On that fateful morning, Gordie had already hopped into his pickup and was hightailing it out the yard ahead of a plume of dust when I flagged him down and asked him what he wanted me to do.

"Oh yeah," he said, removing his Co-Op hat and scratching his white scalp. "Well, why don't you take the B and the hayrack and load them bales from that field I showed you yesterday? That should do you most of the day." He glanced at the sky. "Might rain," he said, and then floored it and was gone, hidden in a cloud of dust before I could yell that I'd not only never driven the Allis-Chalmers B before, but I'd never driven a tractor before. And a car only once or twice.

If you were a steady and dependable kid, the people in my small town would assume that you could handle pretty much anything, which is why I routinely collected bills for Sayler Bros. Hardware, pedaling around town with a couple thousand in cash stuffed in my back pocket every month, ran the projector at the Dakota Theatre five nights a week, and delivered all the newspapers in town.

And that was why Gordie figured I could handle a tractor without too much trouble.

Which proved to be true, at least at the outset. Soon I was proudly standing on the tractor platform getting a feeling for the steering as the little beast bounced over the prairie roads toward my date with destiny, trailing a clattering flatbed hayrack behind. Duck soup, I figured, as I spotted a pair of tractor-sized boulders—you wouldn't want to crash into them with a vehicle—that signaled the entrance to a steep, sloping path choked with marravarich, or stinkweed. I negotiated the narrow way between the boulders and onto the nearly invisible path and nearly killed the little tractor before I goosed the Allis B up the long steep hill on top of which storm clouds seemed to be piling.

But the day was young, the clouds far away, and I was weaving the lies I would tell my friends about what size tractor Gordie had let me drive my second day at work: Maybe a brand-new 5010 John Deere that had just come out, and the factory had asked him to test (he'd tested several products prior to their coming onto the market, although no tractors); or a Minneapolis-Moline G-VI. I certainly didn't want to tell my friends that the first tractor I'd ever driven was a dinky little Allis B, and this was definitely a dinky one, the first Allis B of late-1930s vintage, and seemed not much bigger than a go-cart to a kid who wanted to drive a big tractor. My friends would make fun of me all winter if they ever found out.

The air was soupy and the sweat bees swarming and bumping into my bare back as I pulled off into an alfalfa field. At first I wasn't sure it was the right field, but then I saw the bales. They were small and square because Gordie was too busy to adjust his baler. He said they were the perfect size for one person to haul.

Which was true, I discovered as I idled the B beside a group of bales, tossed them onto the hayrack, climbed up, and hoisted them to their proper positions on the rack, and then drove on to the next group. I felt like a real farmer.

I filled the bottom row, and then most of the second, third, and fourth rows, leaving an area to toss the bales, and a path for me to climb up the rows. Time flew by. Clouds had blotted out the sun long before, and a cool breeze had thankfully sprung up. I had nearly filled all the rows when I paused for a minute to glance at the sky. Instead of puffy clouds or long gentle white ones, the sky had turned variously gun-metal gray, and angry black, and purple as a bruised grape.

While I had worked, the anvil-topped black clouds had clawed miles up into the atmosphere, until now they towered menacingly over me, their hulking weight pressing down ominously on me, dwarfing the hayrack and the Allis and me. All I could say was, "Uh oh." I felt alone and tiny and insignificant.

A white zigzag of lightning sizzled across the sky, followed instantly by a clap of thunder that nearly startled me off the edge of the hayrack. I tried to calmly finish pushing the last bales of the load into their slots as a cold wind surged and the first fat raindrops plopped in the dust and plinked on the Allis.

I scrambled down, climbed onto the cabless tractor, and slowly turned it around, puttering toward the prairie path and home. I knew I was in for a little blow. Had I been wiser or more experienced, I would simply have crawled under the hayrack and waited for it to pass. But Gordie had said something about not wanting those bales to get wet, and, well, I simply didn't know what I was doing.

A hundred yards of driving and the deluge from the skies opened, drenching me instantly in ice-cold rain, and blotting out the landscape around me. It could have been in a blizzard, for all I could see. I was all alone with the gray hissing rain, howling wind, and crackling thunder. I trembled at every flash and noise, and when the hail began pummeling me, I shoved the Allis into high, and decided to outrun the storm.

For a few moments, it was actually fun. To control my terror, I whooped and yelled as though I was on an old-time cattle drive trying to keep the beasts together during the storm. Had anyone seen me, my white-knuckled hands knotted around the steering wheel, black hair streaming behind, teeth gritted, and a maniacal look in my eyes as the rain cascaded around me and pellets of snow-white hail bounced off the hood of the orange Allis, they would have thought me insane. If you have ever been caught unprotected in the open during a prairie storm, you'll know that I probably was, a little bit.

Finally, with whips of white lightning and growls of thunder reverberating around me, I came to my senses. Ozone burned my nostrils as I bounced along the path. I peered behind me into the stinging rain and saw that bales were beginning to jar loose.

But before I could slow, the earth seemed to give way. The front edge of the tractor, the back wheels, and suddenly the entire hayrack was slanting downward and gaining speed. The hill!

I'd forgotten about that long and steep hill I'd climbed up to get to the alfalfa field. There was one other little knell of warning in my brain, but before I could capture it, my attention was pulled back to the tractor.

I was going too fast. I had to slow down. Bales had begun to bounce off the side of the hayrack, disappearing into the torrents of rain and hail. I shoved in the clutch, and tried to downshift. But it wouldn't slip into another gear. Now I was in neutral, and if I had not already been sopping wet, I would have been covered in sweat, because I knew I was in big trouble. The unfettered tractor and hayrack and I picked up amazing speed, plunging wildly down the hill, clanging and clattering and crashing into dips and ruts in the road. I was tossed every which way. My teeth ached from the jarring. Fenceposts were a blur. Bales shot by me on both sides, ejected from the rack. Half the time I was in the air, tethered to the machine only by my deathgrip on the steering wheel.

I had to stop. So I jammed on the brakes. The rear wheels of the Allis locked, and began skidding. I glanced behind me, and the hairs on the nape of my neck prickled. The hayrack had turned almost sideways, and was skidding recklessly towards me, the hitch bent at a "V" where it was attached to the Allis. I felt the front wheels of the Allis lift off the ground. Half the bales were gone, and the others were jouncing around in the rack, seeking an exit.

Lightning smashed into the field not a dozen feet away. The clap of thunder was deafening. The tractor skidded sideways, front wheels in the air like a rearing pony, back wheels gouging out great gouts of wet black dirt and spewing it off to the side.

Then I remembered what my subconscious had been trying to warn me about: the boulders at the entry way to the road I was now careening down. In my mind's eye I could see the tractor pile up against one of the boulders, followed by the hayrack slamming into it, pulverizing the little Allis and me.

I could feel the force of the hayrack behind me, controlling me, and instinctively knew that in seconds the drama would be over: I would soon tip over, or be tossed off and ground under, or smashed into the rock.

So I did the only thing I could do: I released the brakes. For a moment the small tractor and hayrack and I continued sliding sideways down the hill toward the rocks. Then slowly the rear tractor wheels gained purchase, the front end touched earth, and the tractor found the road. In short order, the hayrack followed as though nothing untoward had happened.

There was but one thing to do now, and I did it. I grasped the steering wheel, gritted my teeth, and rode the clattering beast down the rest of the hill. Now I knew how Pecos Bill of myth felt when he rode a tornado. With breathtaking speed, the huge boulders loomed up out of the mist, and then I shot the gap between them, one wheel of the hayrack scraping past them, and across the main road (if another vehicle had been coming, I would have been in pieces small enough for soup, for sure), and onto another grassy road on the other side. I bounced and jounced and rattled, until with judicious use of the brakes, I calmed the beast down, slowed it, and stopped.

And there I sat, trembling, sucking air and blowing as hard as a horse that had been ill-used, while the wind roared and rain washed over my face and the occasional hailstone rapped me on the head. I just sat while lightning crackled overhead and thunder boomed, until I stopped shaking.

Shortly, the worst of the storm blew over. I turned the tractor around and slowly headed between the rocks and back up the hill. Only a few bales remained in the rack. The rest were strewn up and down the hill, and on either side, like casualties of a great war.

The storm clouds blew away, the sun peeped out, and I began picking up the bales and carting them back to the hayrack one by one, until I had it filled.

At supper, Gordie smiled mischievously and asked how my first tractor ride had gone.

"Um, pretty good," I lied. "Except the storm slowed me down a little bit."

"What about that hill? Any trouble?"

"Not really," I lied again. "A little tricky maybe."

"Good, good," he said. "I came home that way, and saw that somebody else had some trouble on that hill," he said. "Judging by how the road was tore up."

I inhaled some soup into the wrong pipe, and spluttered and coughed for a while. When I regained my voice I said, "That is a tricky hill. But other than that, my first day on a tractor was duck soup."

Learning to Drive Tractor

Sis drives the family Farmall cutting hay.

Junior learns to drive tractor under Pa's steady hand in this Oliver advertising painting.

At the wheel
of a Farmall.

With suitable concentration, Junior pilots the family's Avery.

Rust Exposure: How I Found My First Tractor Through a Camera Lens

BY LEE KLANCHER

Lee Klancher has photographed and written about everything from his many motorcycling journeys to the farm tractors that he grew up surrounded by in small-town Wisconsin. He currently makes his home in Austin, Texas, but still travels the country taking pictures and collecting stories about vehicles of all sorts. Lee Klancher's photography has appeared in more than a dozen books and hundreds of magazines, including *Men's Journal*, *Draft*, and *Motorcyclist*. He's the author of *Legendary Farmall Tractors*, among other tractor histories.

"Look, I'm not an intellectual—I just take pictures."
—*Photographer Helmut Newton*

I grew up in a thrice-rennovated salt box of a house located three miles north of the 50 souls who inhabited the town of Brill, Wisconsin. Tractors were simply a part of life in Brill, and they drove past our house pulling hay wagons or manure spreaders nearly every day.

My neighbor Bobby Cherney and his family's John Deeres were regular visitors to the Klancher family spread. He was the same age as I, and would drive the quarter-mile of gravel road from his farm with a tractor at least once a week, sometimes to help my dad out with some task and other times just to visit.

On summer afternoons when I ran out of books to read and the trout were hidden away for the day, I'd hop on the tractor with Bobby and hang out with him at the Cherney farm. Going to his farm was always a dicey proposition at best. We always seemed to plan to do something fun after the work was done. The problem was the work never seemed to be done. I'd agree to help with some onerous task—fixing fences, repairing an implement, or hauling a feed wagon—after which we would plan to ride our motorcycles, watch *The Muppet Show*, or (on special occasions) go to the truck pull at the county fair. Inevitably, we would finish the onerous task and a brother, parent, or catastrophe would cause us to jettison the plan for fun in order to perform another onerous task (like carrying home a freshly-born calf, which is one of my least favorite onerous tasks as it literally bathes you in afterbirth). This hellish cycle typically went on until either we slipped out and suffered retributions or it was time for me to go home.

The endless stream of onerous tasks appears to me to be simply a natural byproduct of farming, much like manure. The situation was compounded by the fact that the Cherney family suffered from a bit of a labor shortage. Bobby's dad worked for the gas company and the responsibility for running the large operation fell on the oldest brother, Gary, and Bobby's mom, Marilyn. She was a tough, hard-working woman, and raising the boys and managing the farm appeared to overwhelm her much of the time. I remember countless tearful Marilyn monologues in which she recounted to me how much work she and her family did, and how hard it was to make ends meet.

As I don't particularly care for onerous tasks or afterbirth, my memories of the farm are anything but idyllic. As I watched the Cherney family put in twelve-hour days and struggle to keep up, I was happy that my father chose to follow in his mother's footsteps and become a teacher rather than take his father's path to dairy farming.

Somewhat to my parent's chagrin, adrenaline-generating machines fascinated me. I loved speed, and destroyed motorcycles, snowmobiles, and later muscle cars with abandon. The tractors that surrounded me at that time didn't attract much of my interest, though my neighborhood cohorts and I did occasionally use them to suit our thrill-seeking ends.

Bobby could pull wheelies with his family's John Deere 3010. One day while my parents were away, I hosted an impromptu lawn tractor race in which several neighborhood kids and myself gathered all the available lawn tractors and turned my lot into a seven-acre track. The lawn was scarred from that for most of the summer, and my dad was disgusted with me for nearly as long. All of this was first-class juvenile entertainment (which I have not quite managed to outgrow). While these are my earliest memories of farm tractors, racing and wheelies have no real relation to my first tractor.

I would find that not on the farm but through the lens of a camera. After high school, I left Brill with no regrets. A small farming community in northern Wisconsin is a wonderful place to grow up, but holds very little attraction for a young man looking to broaden his horizons beyond PeeWee's Tavern, church league softball, and county fair truck pulls.

College suited me, so much so that I took a long and convoluted path finishing my journalism degree at the University of Minnesota. When I did, I was in my mid-20s and had found that telling stories in words and images was more than a profession—it was a passion.

At the ripe age of 24, I was writing travel stories and shooting photos of canoe trips, motorcycle racing, and deer hunting. A local publisher was looking for new writers, and one of the editors knew my work and that I had grown up around farm tractors. He asked me to send in some samples and I was eventually offered a contract to write a book about farm tractors. The money was terrible but the challenge intrigued me. Before I signed the dotted line, I decided to take a few images and see if I could photograph as well write the book.

This Farmall 300 was photographed on a cold, clear October 1993 morning in Minnesota.
Lee Klancher

This image of a hard-working Farmall and the oxen team was taken on a rainy afternoon
at a farm show in Rogers, Minnesota, in 1993. The image was shot on Kodachrome
transparency film with a Minolta XG-7. *Lee Klancher*

The old post fence and backlighting were the draw for this shot of a John Deere 730 and Farmall Super M photographed on October 27, 2009. This high-dynamic range image was created from three exposures taken with a Canon 1DS and a 24mm lens at f/7.1.
Lee Klancher

The steering wheel of Paul C. Klancher's Ford 9N. *Lee Klancher*

I did a little research, and found a farm show in Rogers, Minnesota. In August 1993, I drove a few hours north to the show on a rainy late August Sunday morning and scouted for cleanly restored machines to photograph. I found much more than that.

While squeezing in close to one of the running machines to make a detail photograph, the smell of burnt oil and gasoline exhaust evoked vivid memories of time I spent tinkering on machinery with my late grandfather, Paul C. Klancher. My grandfather had retired from farming before I was born, and he loved mechanical things. His shed was full of old trucks, ATVs, boat motors, and chain saws. He also had a tractor he used to haul wood and work his endlessly expanding network of garden plots.

My grandfather doted on his grandchildren and he indulged my love of internal combustion toys. He would purchase various toys for himself, and then pass them on to me when I was old enough. He bought an ancient Tradewinds Tiger snowmobile and passed it down when he upgraded to a newer model (nearly as old as the Tiger). A neighbor sold him a pair of Indian 100cc dirt bikes for next to nothing. He expected to keep one for himself to run trap lines, but rode it to the end of the driveway and crashed while turning around. That was the end of his motorcycling career, and he gave both motorcycles to me.

When I think of my grandfather, I remember a gregarious, generous, and occasionally gruff man in denim overalls surrounded by battered wooden boxes that housed his clevis pins, wrenches, and rifles. He had a mildly nefarious nature, friends with nicknames such as Pluto and Wild Bill, loved to play cards, and liked to slip five dollar bills into his grandchildren's pockets. A smokehouse built of old barn wood comes to mind, as does a red shed with peeling paint where he sharpened his lawn mower blades, oiled his muskrat traps, and built shelves for my grandmother. His life had a simple authenticity that rings true to me, and I still enjoy going back to his home.

What I found at the show was that farm tractors could connect me to my grandfather. That smell of hot oil and old iron evokes this man. His memory was present while I photographed these old machines, and I dedicated the book to him. I still think of him often when I am around old tractors.

In addition to discovering a connection to my grandfather, I found one of my favorite images of a farm tractor at the Rogers show. I was looking to take just one decent photograph while at the show. I knew that doing so was nearly impossible with all the machines lined up in neat, closely spaced rows. A beat-up Farmall draped in chains, rust, and cobbled parts provided an opportunity. The tractor was parked in an open patch of grass next to a field where several costumed men were plowing with an ox. I liked the juxtaposition of the Farmall and the animal it replaced, so I made a photograph with the tractor in the foreground. At the time, I expected little from the image due to the low light and battered condition of the tractor.

As time passed, the image became one of my favorites. The well-worn tractor evoked a lifetime of labor, and the misty, damp light added a somber tone. This wasn't farming in which young boys wave gleefully from the back of their shiny machine; this image showed the rugged back-breaking farming life I understood from my childhood.

My education in tractor appreciation was hardly over. In fact, I don't believe I even understood what I discovered. I just continued to make images.

At the farm show in Rogers, I made a connection with Minnesota-based collector Greg Thune. He owned several nicely restored tractors, a McCormick-Deering 10-20 and a steel-wheeled Farmall F-12. I photographed them at his Minnesota farm on a sun-drenched evening in September 1993. Along with his restored machines, Greg had several dozen parts tractors rusting away in his yard and fields. The light was beautiful, and I made some shots of the 10-20 glowing in the light with the rusted equipment in the foreground.

I photographed his F-12 in his pasture. As the evening sun warmed and richened, I was drawn to the remains of a Farmall enveloped in daisies. I shot a photograph of the steering wheel of the rusty machine on a whim. The old iron and nice light drew me in, and I made a half-dozen shots of the derelict machine.

My next subject was the 300 owned by Don Thune. On a cold, crisp morning in October 1993, I drove up to Don's farm as the day's first light was bouncing off a fresh coat of frost on the ground.

A brisk wind blowing across the open fields near Don's farm was bone-chilling. We drove his clean, sharp 300 out to a spot in the field and

I shot a roll of images as quickly as possible. Don wore a tan Carhartt jacket stained with years of hard work. I liked the jacket very much, and took several exposures of Don on the tractor.

The images from those early photo shoots made a tremendous impact on me and my photography. The battered tractor in bad light, the rusty steering wheel, and the early light on Don's jacket all evoke my grandfather's time.

My love of photographing abandoned tractors led me to photograph *The Tractor in the Pasture*, a photo-essay that shows old iron abandoned in pastures from around the United States and beyond.

I continued to pursue my interest in tractors, and have photographed hundreds of tractors for books and calendars. Each time I make a photograph, I'm looking for a natural, gritty element. Weathered wood, rusty iron, and peeling paint all draw my eye. You'll find these elements in most of my favorite images, whether they are of pristinely restored farm tractors, a brand-new Victory motorcycle, or the owner of a brewery.

I also finally took at least part ownership of a tractor. My grandfather's Ford 9N became increasingly cranky over the years, and refused to start once it was warmed up. The engine most likely needs an overhaul. After being forced to leave the tractor out in the woods time after time, my father, uncle, and family friend Sam decided to buy a new tractor with a bucket rather than fix the Ford.

We all pitched in and bought a nice clean little Farmall 240 with a bucket. That tractor served us well in all kinds of tasks. The Farmall sees limited use these days as Sam bought a Kubota four-wheel-drive.

Grandpa's Ford sits in the shed. We tried to sell it without much effort about ten years ago, but no one took us up on the ad I posted and we've all lost interest in selling it. I find some comfort in seeing it in the shed each time I'm back visiting, and hope that it never does get sold. Someday, perhaps, I'll restore that old tractor. I think I would enjoy that, and suspect that the hands-on work would make that Ford my first tractor.

But that won't be happening anytime soon. Until I crack the engine of my grandfather's Ford and dig in, my first farm tractor is a visual expression of nostalgia I found in three photo shoots that took place in the fall of 1993.

8N-Joyment

BY GERARD W. RINALDI

Gerard Rinaldi is the publisher of *9N-2N-8N Newsletter* and a devoted Ford N Series tractor fan. His magazine is a stylish and informative club newsletter that keeps members up to date on all things relating to Ford tractors.

In this essay, Gerard describes how the restoration and use of his Ford 8N tractor taught him new things about himself.

What exactly are the pleasures of owning an old tractor, in keeping it running well, and looking good? When I'm up in the operator's seat, letting my forty-six-year-old machine do what it does best, that's when I contemplate that question.

First of all, the seat of almost any tractor is a place unbelievably conducive to meditating, if you haven't yet realized it. Perhaps one day I'll offer a sequel to Robert Pirsig's popular novel. Will there be a call for *Zen and the Art of Tractor Maintenance?*

It takes some concentration to keep the old tractors running, but not too much. They seem to oblige with an unusual willingness to perform, and with a constitution not often found in many of our products today—they never featured planned obsolescence. It still pleasantly surprises me each time my old Ford 8N leaps to attention, like an old dog who is ready for a romp despite any ills of age, even in the dead of winter.

In our ambience of bubble-pack, squash-down, throw-away living, there is both a convenience and a bolstered economy in which we all benefit somehow. It is a curious game of paradox.

But there is another game I enjoy as well. To win, one must perform the trick of keeping the oldest things useful and working well for the longest time by the most energy-efficient and cost-effective means. That's marathon talk. The real competition is with oneself, to get in shape, to maintain that tone, to plan ahead, to work carefully and efficiently, and to pace all efforts. With such an attitude, I restored a tractor and depend on its usefulness today.

These thoughts go back more than thirty years, when I began teaching art subjects in the public school of a community that was still quite rural. Although it would change, haying was active on several small farms nearby, supporting the many horse enthusiasts. One of my students, David, a high schooler unusually well informed about tractors, had an uncanny ability to name the make and model from great distances when only a tiny portion of the machine could be seen.

He began to teach me. His father, Tom, owned an old Allis-Chalmers B, and I was invited to come over for a demonstration, a test ride, and my first opportunity to cut a field on a real tractor. To say that I was unhitched would be an understatement. It was one of those sudden and total fascinations that I preferred not to have explained to me. I only wanted to savor it. I wanted a tractor of my own, though I had no reason, no farm, to justify such an acquisition.

David and I, sometimes his dad and one or two of the other kids, would set out after school now and then, to visit a dealer or a farm. There were long, long conversations about the merits and failings of this or that as we aired our curiosities. There were more opportunities to drive. On my desk, a small collection of sales literature and farm magazines germinated. My vocabulary and my focus about tractors began to resolve. Had I become re-hitched?

One day, an acquaintance called from one of the horse farms. He knew of a tractor that had been in a fire several months before, and it had been towed out to the junk pile to decompose. David and I went right over to see it. He identified it as a Ford 8N with a lift system originally designed by Harry Ferguson. He began to describe each lever and function.

We decided that the fire burned intensely hot but briefly—a gas tank leak probably. All rubber, composition, or light metal had burned or melted, but in its haste to pass, the fire had left the inner machine intact. It might run again, this 8N, although the completely rusted remains tried to conceal this secret. We were excited about the challenge, and David promised to help.

I offered to buy it. The man said, "Take it." We rushed to David's house to borrow the front wheels from the Allis-Chalmers B, then back to our heap to mount them. We towed it out of the junk and into the field. The seals looked good. Each move was a gesture of promise.

We waited for late evening to minimize encounters with traffic, then towed that tractor twenty-eight miles back to my house. Our excitement would not subside although it was now past midnight. We just had to put it on blocks…just begin some disassembly…just the front grille…just these old burnt wires…just this…just that….

Before long we had removed enough parts so that we needed to establish an order for storing them, and some notes for the resplendent days of reassembly that were ahead. Until then, we would take apart all but the inner engine and transmission.

Next day we got some cardboard boxes to organize the parts removal and went off to the Ford dealer to look at parts books and service manuals. We mapped out a plan for what had to be replaced or rebuilt. Would it be easy to get parts for a then twenty-year-old tractor?

No problem! In David's file cabinet were the names and numbers of used parts dealers all over the country. Instead, in our next visit to our dealer, we told him of our project, and I offered to buy the parts from him if he would coach us through the difficult tasks.

Again, no problem! Many old tractors are well-supported with replacements, unlike car parts, which become exhausting to locate once a vehicle becomes ten to fifteen years old. Today, although some of the 9Ns are nearly sixty years old, Ford—now New Holland—supports over 90 percent of available parts replacement.

Restoring an old tractor or implement is more a matter of attitude than task. The hours passed during take-down, wire brushing, repainting, and rebuilding are a vague entity hidden by the absorbing enjoyment of deciding to do it, and measuring the progress. It is possible to sense the engineering integrity.

In re-assembly there is a strength greater than new, it seems. But my favorite discovery was quite unexpected. When I had begun to operate my 8N six months later, I was certain I could feel every single part that I had touched, working both in an aggregate unity and separately as well.

The drawings in the manuals, the connections of all the parts to each other, their entire articulation, had become a tactile reality. I felt it in the steering, at the clutch, in the seat under me, and in the sounds and smells. Since then and over these many years, I have known exactly and immediately which part was feeling a strain, which part would need a service. Every operator should have to restore a machine to improve operating skills and senses. One then operates in such a way to deliberately protect each part.

I had no uses for my 8N, though. No farm, no big tract of land. My family and neighbors all wondered what I would do with it. It was enough for me just to have it, to like it, and to drive it around. I felt a pride in bringing it back to life, and the tractor itself was living proof.

One day, I received an invitation to drive it in a 4th of July parade. I had been giving the kids rides in the trailer, so why not? Then, more serious ideas began to occur. The old Wagner loader was a perfect tool for lifting bundles of shingles up to the roof, saving my energy for the roofing job itself. Then a stone wall was needed to enhance the landscaping. What a backsaver, that 8N! When I realized I could actually dig for the foundation of a new carport myself, it was thrilling. I could bring in the firewood! I could help a neighbor whose car was stuck in mud. It was easy to fell a tree in a specific direction. And so, my lifelong dependence had begun.

One day I recognized that my tractor knew how to help itself. A rear tire had gone flat. It was filled with calcium solution and impossibly heavy for me. I blocked the axle, removed the tire, and carefully, so it wouldn't fall, rolled it forward to chain it to the loader. Then I lifted it into the air and backed my pickup under it, lowered it, and went to the repair place. When I returned, I reversed the operation. Simple!

My son and nephews all learned to drive it from about age eight. As high schoolers, they put it to use in their summertime business to earn college expenses. We found a York rake and took jobs building driveways, parking areas, and lawns. The boys even enjoyed giving the 8N another cleaning and repainting.

Then I bought another tractor, a 2N, with a better loader, intending to refurbish both and to switch the better loader to my 8N. Both tractor and loader were badly rusted and had some worn parts, but that's been restored also. In fact, I've now restored four tractors, three loaders, a flail knife mower, a York rake, a spreader, a snowblower, two rear blades, and a trailer. The task has become so easy because it is so rewarding.

Today, I can't imagine how I might have done without my fabulous Ford 8N. Teasingly, my family tells everyone that I won't even think about going on vacation unless I can bring the 8N.

I was so excited about it that I began to publish the *9N-2N-8N Newsletter*, a homespun quarterly intended for N-nuts like me. We are mesmerized by the spirit of these great old tractors, and devoted to preserving them and their history.

These old Fords are so evenly tempered, so forgiving in use, so simple to knock down in a few strokes that even a novice can change a part. They are so practical to own and use, and so efficient at doing what they were designed to do, and so subtly beautiful in their Art Deco motif, and so inspiring to a pride of ownership, and so refreshingly unlike so many of the throw-away things of today.

Now, as my subscribers exchange their questions and answers, and tell their N-stories, I learn new things nearly every day from all over the country. My 8N has been like a school or a special door opening to experiences, pleasures, and associations I never imagined I could have.

The Young Pedal-Tractor Farmer

Junior sits proudly at the wheel of his Murray pedal tractor.

a Merry Christmas

Dick Martin

1964

EXCLUSIVE *Ertl*

LIVE ACTION SCALE MODEL TOYS THAT SELL

DESIGNED TO THE EXACTING STANDARDS OF THE WORLD'S FINEST MANUFACTURERS

A Mayoral Tractor

BY JOHN DIETZ

The former mayor of Memphis, Richard Hackett was raised in the suburbs we know as the Graceland area and handled the funeral co-ordination for Elvis Presley. He got his first tractor in 1980 to help with managing some land he purchased. He still has that tractor today—and he still finds it helpful, as well as therapeutic.

The mayor of Memphis, young Dick Hackett, received a very special delivery at his acreage in 1985—a shiny new mid-size Ford 1710 four-wheel-drive tractor. It was his first tractor. He still operates it, 25 years and 2,400 engine-hours later, although both he and the 'old blue' are semi-retired.

Twice, Hackett gained national recognition, first as the coordinator of the Elvis Presley funeral in 1977, and then in December 1982, at age 33, when he became the youngest mayor of a major U.S. city. Today, he is the chief executive officer of the private, not-for-profit Children's Museum of Memphis.

Hackett, at 60, is a prime example of a city-guy who loves the rural life and his farm tractor.

Born in 1949, Hackett grew up in a Memphis suburb. It was known then as Whitehaven; today it has a more familiar name.

"I actually grew up on the west side of Graceland," Hackett says. "When I moved out of home, I lived in the Graceland subdivision. Both places were less than a mile from the Graceland mansion, one on the west side and one on the east side. The actual Graceland mansion is probably four blocks from our family home."

Whitehaven was about two miles north of the Mississippi state line. Some of the best bass fishing in the South could be found in a farm pond down the road about 12 miles south from Whitehaven. In the late 1960s, Richard Hackett used to go down there to fish. The pond covered about 10 acres. Near the pond, there were tall cypress and willow trees. On the higher ground, oak and other hardwood trees flourished.

It was a pretty, quiet area where a boy or young adult could get in touch with nature. Hackett, however, wasn't the only one to enjoy the pond. A young Memphis rock-n-roll start, Elvis, purchased the farm and its pond for his bride, Priscilla. He renamed it as the Circle G Ranch.

Hackett recalls, "The Circle G is probably two miles from my house now, by coincidence. Bass, I probably caught more bass off that lake than any other lake in my life, for sure I did!"

Hackett enrolled in Memphis State College in the late 1960s. His triple major was education, psychology and social welfare.

"When I was in college, I coached Little League Baseball for a while. Because I had met Elvis, and particularly his dad, Vernon, they sponsored a team called Elvis Presley Enterprises. I coached it; they paid for the sponsorship. When we won the league championship one year, Elvis gave all the boys an autographed baseball. He was down to earth, very easy to talk to."

About the time Hackett was finishing college, Memphis elected a new mayor—J. Wyeth Chandler. Chandler hired Hackett as his assistant in 1972, before Hackett graduated from college. "I stayed with him until 1978. Being his executive assistant allowed me to cross lines and be involved in all divisions and departments of city government," he says.

After coordinating the Elvis funeral in August 1977, Hackett ran for his first public office, Shelby County Clerk. He was elected in 1978 and 1982.

Only weeks after the county re-election, Mayor Chandler resigned prematurely. Chandler had been appointed as a state judge. In the special election that followed, voters chose Hackett to fill out the 13-month term as mayor. He was elected twice after that, in 1983 and 1987. Hackett lost the historic 1991 election for mayor of Memphis by only 141 votes. His successor was W. W. Herenton, the first African-American mayor in the city's history.

Hackett worked for two non-profit agencies over the next 15 years. In July 2006, he became the CEO/director of the Children's Museum of Memphis.

LIFESTYLE CHANGE

Hacket and his wife, Kathy, were starting a country life even as he was serving as mayor. They were about to change lifestyle. They needed the tractor to renovate some property they had purchased a bit south of Memphis, in DeSoto County, Mississippi, close to his old fishing hole. The 30-horsepower tractor came with three attachments, a disc, bush hog and loader.

"I needed it for bush-hogging mostly and a little box-blading work," he says. Typically, a bush hog is a heavy-duty rotary mower. It attaches to a tractor's three-point hitch and is driven by the power take-off. The blades will whack their way through dense vegetation, making the bush hog a good tool for clearing mixed brush, grass and even small trees.

Dick and Kathy owned 11 acres and had secured an option to purchase more land when it became available. Once fixed up, it would be the place to raise their family.

"It was an old pasture that had rolling hills and some old farm houses. They don't exist anymore," he says. "Eventually, I acquired the entire 150 acres, and I maintain all that with my tractors. We have two now. We've been able to rear three children on the farm. We have chicken coops and about 75 chickens today. We have four dogs right now, and have had as many as six."

It is called Brush-Hill Farm, in honor of his parents.

"It's named after the place my parents lived when they were first married in Nashville, on the Cumberland River. They lived on Brush-Hill Road. When Dad died, we named it Brush Hill Farm to make Momma feel more comfortable. She moved over to be with us, and said that her address was still Brush-Hill Farm."

There is a deep family attachment now to the rural home in northeastern Mississippi, situated in one of the fastest growing counties in the United States.

"Our daughter, Mary Shea, and her husband live on it. Our oldest son, Jason, and his wife live on it. Our youngest son, William, now is a law student at the University of Memphis. He will have an opportunity to have a house here, too," Hackett says.

Thinking back on the history of that now 25-year-old tractor, Hackett recalls the day it was delivered. "When it was delivered, Ford had someone stay with me, going over the operating manual and showing me the do's and don'ts, the why's and why-not's and things like how to put attachments on. No, I had not operated heavy equipment before. It was all new."

Getting comfortable on it required some practice, a few rides.

"The fellow who sold it to me was somewhat my senior. He always said it's like swimming. Don't ever get too comfortable with it. He cautioned me about the dangers, particularly with a bush hog, and the dangers of being on a hill. It was at a later date that I got the front end loader for it."

Gradually, while serving the city, the youthful mayor slowly worked at developing his own little haven. More than once, his tractor was stuck.

He recalls, "Doing some of the lower land, there's some soft spots to watch. You'd wait a few days after a rain, and finally think it would be fine to bush-hog. Suddenly, you'd hit a soft spot and it would just literally suck that tractor down into the ground. Eventually, I had a winch mounted on it, on the front, at the recommendation of the dealer. They recommend against bush-hogging without someone being at home, but if you are by yourself, it's good to have a winch on it."

On weekends and evenings, still serving as mayor, Dick Hackett could be found out on the hillsides of his own retreat.

He says, "I was the only one that put hours on the tractor. It kind of became my toy. It was and is therapy, if you will. It gives me a chance to get away from the entire world, out there in the fields, bush-hogging or whatever."

He adds, "Over the years, I probably have scared up more than my share of coyotes. Multiple times, I've certainly scared up deer on the property. That's always a treat. We have white tail deer here. I sometimes had deer in my yard when I was growing up, like I do now. It's always a treat to see a deer, or even a herd of deer."

That tractor has done thousands of hours of site beautification for Brush-Hill Farms. Hackett says, "We spent months pushing dead trees into ditches, and weeks dragging out areas that were in beans and corn. We cleaned nearly three miles of walking trails and five acres of manicured lawn space. We built or rebuilt four ponds. We have three that are three to five acres in size and one that is a 15 acre lake for duck hunting!"

Hackett recently added a larger tractor to help him manage the more developed property. The newer tractor is a large, rear-wheel-drive New Holland. Attachments include a rotary mower, rotary tiller, a box blade, three-bottom plow, a planter, several side disc implements, a six-foot harrow for leveling and a three-point lift boom. The boom is handy for odd jobs, such as lifting and moving a large tree. The larger tractor today does the heavier work, such as discing and field preparation.

The Hacketts do several acres of mowing today with a set of 360-degree, zero-turn lawn mowers. They manicure lawn grass around each house and a fenced-in yard area for the dogs.

"We put in three gardens for three households," Dick Hackett says. "We also have sunflower fields, soybean fields and fields for feeding deer. As for the harvesting, well, everything we do is for feed plots for the animals. They take the crop, and we enjoy the lifestyle!"

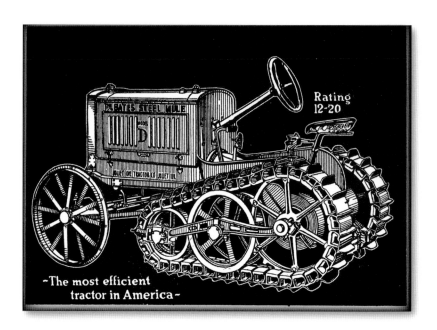

Rating
12-20

-The most efficient
tractor in America~

One Author's Beginnings

BY DON MACMILLAN

Englishman Don Macmillan is the dean of John Deere historians. Don has been involved in all aspects of vintage and new farm tractors: He started as a farmer before becoming a Deere dealer and has since become a well-known collector of vintage tractors and involved with the English branch of the Two-Cylinder Club. His books include the landmark *John Deere Tractors and Equipment*, volumes one and two, *John Deere Albums* volumes one and two, and *John Deere Tractors Worldwide*.

In this reminiscence, Don pays homage to the tractors that have influenced his life.

In the late 1930s, I was working on a 640-acre Cotswold farm, ten miles (16 km) from Gloucester, where we had one Allis-Chalmers B tractor. All of the rest of the work was done with horses, as well as the annual visit of the steam threshing outfit.

I learnt to plow with three horses and a two-furrow walking plow—no sulky plows in the United Kingdom in those days!—milk cows by hand as we had two herds, one a pedigree Friesian, make ricks of sheaves and thatch them against our wet weather, build stone walls, and shear sheep. It was bad luck on the sheep.

When World War II began, we were ordered to plow up more land, so we ordered a new Allis-Chalmers WF, similar to one we borrowed occasionally from a brother-in-law. The farmer's brother had a son who knew his tractors; he had ordered a John Deere AR.

Both tractors were a long time coming, and in the end the brother was offered a Minneapolis-Moline U, which he accepted. Almost at once the AR turned up in Gloucester, so he phoned us to see if we would like it. My boss agreed that if it would pull three furrows up a steep bank we were about to reclaim, we would have it.

When the dealer brought it out to our farm, I was delegated to do the demonstration, a task it performed easily. Not only did it pull the three-furrow Cockshutt plow with ease, I even persuaded the farmer subsequently to buy a four-furrow. Everyone was amazed at the pulling power of this relatively small tractor when compared with the local 15-30 and W-30 International models popular locally. So instead of a commitment to the orange, I became an enthusiast for the green and yellow.

Despite this change of allegiance, there was another pull towards the orange, one that started my second chief interest in my farming life. We were one of the first farms to have a combine harvester, a five-foot-cut (150-cm) Allis-Chalmers 60 PTO-driven bagger of the early type with the round-top to the straw-walker hood. Again the AR proved as good on the PTO as the drawbar.

On the gas tank of the new tractor it said John Deere, Moline, Illinois. So I wrote to John Deere, Moline, Illinois, and said what a fabulous tractor we had with the AR. They wrote back and said when the war is over you must come and visit.

In the fall of 1947, I made the first of some twenty-three trips so far to the United States, visiting all the major tractor makers in addition to my visit to Moline, Waterloo, and Dubuque. I visited Allis-Chalmers, Caterpillar, International, and M-M; of the major manufacturers I missed out only on Oliver.

Prior to this, in August 1942, I had started contract plowing on my own account through the British War Agricultural Committees. It proved impossible to find a secondhand John Deere, so I bought an Oliver 90 on rubbers, a Ransomes four-furrow plow, and a fuel tender with a rear platform for my motorcycle.

I was sent initially to Chipping Camden in Gloucestershire, but the heavy clay ground proved impossible to plow, even with steel wheels on the Oliver, or for the War Ag's crawlers, so after a trip to Dorset where the ground was the same, I ended up in Wiltshire where I have been ever since. I had so much work for my outfit, machinery being scarce, that I ordered a new John Deere D, and on February 8, 1943, I became the proud owner of serial number 154757, my first John Deere, for £415 on steels, about $1,660. With another driver, we were inundated with work, and farmers asked me, as a contractor journeying about, to find them different machines.

In 1944, I bought my first combine, my second love after John Deere tractors, a Case QRS 12-foot (360-cm) bagger with the C engine. Again, so much combining was booked that I had to buy a second, an M-M JR 6-foot (180-cm) PTO machine that we pulled with the D. By then I had four John Deere tractors: another used unstyled D, a used unstyled BW, and a new A that was delivered just before harvest on steels, which we used to pull the Case.

After harvest, I decided I could not afford to keep two combines and advertised the M-M for sale. As soon as it was sold, for £10 more than it had cost, I was inundated with requests for combines. I even sold the Case as well, having discovered that I could purchase machines just before using them and sell them afterwards for a profit. And so started my career as a dealer.

Early in 1947, before my trip to the United States, I purchased a 220-acre arable farm to occupy the contracting staff when they were not busy. Two years later, a grass drier (dehydrator) was installed in the barn, and made farming more interesting in the summertime. We harvested special grasses and alfalfa from May to the late fall.

During the 1947 American trip, the directors of Jack Olding and Frank Standen, importers of John Deere machines for the south and east of England respectively, both purchased a new 55 12-foot (360-cm) combine with sacker attachment. When these both became secondhand in

1953, I purchased them, converting one to a tanker for use on my farm. I still own both, and they are with a friend who hopes to restore one out of the two.

My first visit to the United States was in the company of Olding's directors on the way over. We flew in an American Airlines Super Constellation, a four-engined plane with triple tailfin, calling at Shannon in Ireland for dinner, and at Gander for refuelling. Leaving London at 3:30 p.m., we arrived next morning in New York about 8:00.

In order to see one of the new 55 self-propelled combines at work, I had to travel from Moline to Champaign, Illinois, and spend the day with the local Deere dealer and two brothers who owned the machine.

In the evening, waiting at the bus station for a bus to Peoria, I got into a conversation with a guy who had married an English girl from Charlton, near Kingsbridge in Devon. She was the daughter of a pub owner there, a hostelry I knew!

Nothing for it but I must go home with him to meet his wife. In the end, I stayed the night, and they and two friends took me to Peoria the next day in their Packard. Further it was the big football game the next weekend between Illinois and Minnesota, and so I must go down again from Chicago for the weekend. It was all an enjoyable interlude in my six-week tour.

Instead of returning home on the Queen Elizabeth, and due entirely to the great hospitality of all I met, I delayed a week and joined the Queen Mary. This too was fortunate as Frank Standen and his son, Peter, were on the same ship, and it was then I learnt they had arranged to import the second 55 for a farmer in Huntingdonshire.

By 1948, I was operating eight combines and three pickup balers on custom work in addition to my own harvest. After the pound sterling was devalued against the dollar in 1950 from $4 to the pound to $2.80, all Deere machines became too expensive to import. One result of this was that we never had the Numbered Series of two-cylinder tractors in the United Kingdom.

In the year 1958, I sold 112 combines, mostly used, possibly a record for one person, and for several years I passed the eighty mark. In the same year I was appointed the first John Deere dealer in the United Kingdom.

In the context of combines, during my second visit to the United States in 1959, I was able to purchase one of the new 95 Hi-Lo tanker combines. I wanted one with a 12-foot (360-cm) cut, but was told the smallest available was 14-foot (420-cm). By searching various books, I was able to point out that, by ordering a combine with draper header less the pickup unit, and adding a 55 12-foot cutting mechanism, the problem was solved.

Bob Lovett of the Intercontinental division reminded me on many other visits about buying a combine Deere personnel didn't know existed! Incidentally, he was the person who met me off the Zephyr from Chicago in reunion. Again, I still own the 95, and it is with the same friend in Suffolk awaiting restoration.

The reason for my visit in 1959 was the last great show of two-cylinder 30 Series tractors and machinery put on by Deere at Marshalltown, Iowa. I was able to drive an 830 with six-furrow drawn plow with hydraulic lift, and appreciated the potential of this largest and last of the two-cylinder line.

It was here that Deere introduced the 8010 and its eight-furrow integral plow to the amazement (and confusion?) of the farmers present. With its wide sweep when the plow was raised, stewards were necessary at each end of the field to protect the crowd. Finally, everyone wondered what this strange new model-numbering system—eight zero ten zero—meant?

In addition to the tractors, the new Hi-Lo combines were shown for the first time, plus a new small self-propelled Model 40 with either an 8- or 10-foot (240- or 300-cm) grain head, or as working with a two-row corn head.

At home in January 1959, I had bought two tractors that were to become the nucleus of my collection of vintage John Deeres, using them for many years on my farm. The only Model R imported to the British Isles, serial number 4661, was delivered by the importers to a contractor in Dublin, and I managed to purchase it as its second owner. While in Ireland, I also bought a Model M, serial number 14021, several of which were delivered over there, though none came to the United Kingdom.

Three other tractors that I purchased in 1962 in Ireland, two of them new, that were not originally imported to the United Kingdom, but were sent to the Emerald Isle, were John Deere-Lanz 500s, the first John Deere

New Generation model produced in Mannheim, Germany, from January 1960, eight months before the Dallas, Texas, announcement.

It was also in 1962 that the 4010 and 5010 tractors were announced at the December Smithfield Show in London, giving us new John Deere tractors to sell for the first time since 1950.

Over the years, I was able to build up my collection to over thirty tractors including a Waterloo Boy N and a spoke D, both purchased in Canada. Other nice tractors I found for my collection were an unstyled L, serial number 621777, from Michigan, and the only BNH I have on my JD register.

After twenty-two years as a Deere dealer and with a depression signaled, I decided to retire in 1980, and sold my two dealerships to my neighboring Deere dealer. In order to sell all the two-cylinder parts, which I had acquired when Standens gave up John Deere due to lack of supply of new machines, and also the transport vehicles not required by the new owner, I called a sale, with the vintage collection as the draw.

In England, one can put a reserve price on any machines in a sale in case it doesn't make the required price. I had intended selling a few of the tractors and keeping most of the others, but in the event the sale was so good that I only ended up with ten left, plus four others still in North America awaiting shipment.

These fourteen provided the nucleus for a second collection that again mounted into the high twenties, most of which were loaned to our Science Museum, and kept at their storage place on a local disused aerodrome for all the largest items not required at headquarters in London. Eventually the museum lost its curator, and the director of transport, who replaced him, decided they had too many tractors of one make; so I sold all but four to other collectors, as I had nowhere to store them by then.

This brings me to my retirement and the 1980s. A couple of albums on John Deere tractors for Allan Condie in the United Kingdom sparked the thought in a friend's mind, when asked by people at the American Society of Agricultural Engineers, "Did he know anyone who would be interested in writing the history of John Deere Tractors and Equipment?" He kindly thought of me.

Another trip to the United States early in 1988, to ASAE head office in Michigan, a meeting in Moline with Deere vice-president Chet

Lascelles in the chair, and their marketing director, librarian, archivist, ex-editor of *The Furrow*, and ourselves present, resulted in the necessary approval to proceed.

When asked the final question—why the largest farm machinery company in the world, and American to boot, was agreeing to an Englishman writing their history—Chet said simply, "Welcome aboard." I had been aboard for the previous forty-eight years. And now as I write this, and am in the middle of my fourth book, this time for Voyageur Press, the score has risen to fifty-seven.

Homemade Tractor

BY JERRY APPS

Jerry Apps is one of Wisconsin's finest folk historians. He grew up on a farm in the Chain O' Lakes region of Wisconsin, a background that has inspired his writing and his numerous books, including *Barns of Wisconsin, Rural Wisdom: Time-Honored Values of the Midwest, Cheese: The Making of a Wisconsin Tradition, Breweries of Wisconsin*, and *One-Room Country Schoolhouse: History and Recollections from Wisconsin*.

The closest book to his heart may be his collection of childhood reminiscences entitled *When Chores Were Done: Boyhood Stories*, which chronicles his farm youth. His writing is sentimental yet also realistic in describing both the joys and the hardships of life on the farm.

This chapter from *When Chores Were Done* tells of a neighborhood genius who built a farm tractor with his bare hands using the remains of old trucks, spare parts cannibalized from other machinery, and his own down-home know-how.

Pa had a letter from the County Agricultural Agent saying he was eligible to buy a new tractor but there just weren't any because of the war. The demand was too great, and the number of tractors too small.

One day Pa stopped at Jim Colligan's shop in Wild Rose. Colligan was a welder-blacksmith, a kind of jack-of-all-trades who repaired farm equipment, sharpened plow points, and welded things together. Colligan wasn't a big man, not as tall as Pa, but he had the broadest shoulders I'd ever seen and the thickest arms. He was an inventor of sorts, cobbling together old things to make new things. Pa and Jim had been friends for many years—they had known each other since they were kids. They talked about the shortage of farm tractors.

"Been thinking about making a tractor," Jim said.

"How might you do that?" Pa asked.

"Well," Jim said. "Chet Hansel just bought himself a new truck and his old Model A Ford truck is still in pretty good shape. I was thinking of making a tractor out of it."

And that's what he did. He shortened the truck's frame. In place of regular truck tires, he acquired a pair of huge old tires that the county discarded from one of its snowplows. Colligan bolted these tires to the truck wheels and left them flat, to provide more traction for the tractor. With some sheet metal, he fashioned a hood to cover the engine, and he made a seat for the operator to sit on. He covered the whole thing with aluminum paint and drove it out to the farm one summer day in 1942.

What a beauty. I was eight years old and knew I was surely not old enough to drive this fine machine. But right then I looked forward to riding on it, along with my father.

Pa climbed on and made a couple of spins around the farmyard grinning like a Cheshire cat that had just caught a bumblebee. This was the first time he'd ever owned a tractor. Ever. He never showed much emotion, but this day it was obvious that he looked forward to sitting on this tractor and plowing, cutting grain, discing, and dragging. The tractor would make these tasks much easier compared to driving horses. Since he was a young lad, he had followed behind a team, usually walking as the team pulled a plow, a disc, or a drag. Now he could ride, and he would be ahead of the dust for a change, rather than walking in it. This was particularly true when working with a sixteen-foot-wide drag used to smooth ground before planting. The drag teeth, only three or four inches long, stirred up a considerable dust, particularly if the soil happened to be a little dry. Our sandy farm was usually dry, so dust was a part of many farm operations.

Though the tractor was truly wonderful and would soon have a great influence on how we farmed, it had its faults. The mechanical brakes were not good. It took great strength to push the brake pedal enough to engage them, particularly if the tractor happened to be on a rather steep hill. The tractor's transmission was, of course, a truck's transmission. Tractors must move only two or three miles per hour when doing heavy jobs like plowing, pulling rocks, or discing. The transmission had four speeds. Dual low, low, second, and high. Only dual low was slow enough and powerful enough for farm work. In high gear, the former truck reached speeds of forty-five or fifty miles an hour. With the larger than normal tires on the back, the machine moved even faster. Pa laid down the law early. "Whoever drives this tractor will never, ever, put it in high gear. You'll kill yourself and probably somebody else." At the moment, he was talking to himself since he was the only person on the farm who knew how to drive this new invention.

Second gear was also too fast for farm work, but might occasionally be used to drive to and from the fields, if the person was careful. Low was too fast for any heavy farm work, but could be used for such light jobs as toting an empty wagon or maybe pulling a drag.

Early in the fall, Pa hooked the tractor to his new David Bradley double-bottomed plow. It plowed two twelve-inch furrows at a time. The tractor's four-cylinder engine putted as ribbons of freshly turned soil stretched across the twenty-acre field.

"Works like a charm," Pa said that night when he drove the shiny silver tractor into the shed and pulled shut the doors. "Cuts through alfalfa sod like butter."

Frank and Charlie, our draft horses that ordinarily pulled the plow, grazed quietly in the corner of the barnyard. They were growing fat and soft from lack of work.

That October, when we began digging potatoes, Pa said it was my turn to learn how to drive the tractor. Chain O' Lake School dismissed for two weeks of potato vacation so all the kids could help with the potato harvest. Some schools in the state had a spring vacation. Not Chain O' Lake. We had potato vacation in the fall when every man, boy, woman, and girl helped with the harvest so we could finish before the first killing frost ruined the crop.

Pa dropped the draw pin through the tongue of the steel-wheeled wagon, hooking it firmly to the tractor. Earlier he'd sawed several feet off the tongue because hooked to a tractor the tongue could be much shorter than when he used the team. He piled the wagon high with empty one-bushel wooden potato crates, and we drove out to the potato field. Pa hired Weston Coombes to help fork the potatoes out of the ground, and Weston and I sat on the wagon, our feet dangling over the side and kicking into the dirt when we wanted to.

My job was to pick up potatoes that Pa and Weston dug. They marched backwards, side by side across the field, each digging two rows of potatoes with six-tine barn forks. I followed along with a five-gallon pail, picking up the potatoes and dumping my full pail into one of the wooden boxes that we'd strung out across the twenty-acre field.

I still hadn't driven the tractor and wondered what Pa meant when he said today was the day I would learn. As noon approached, Pa stopped digging and suggested we load the filled boxes and haul them to the potato cellar near the chicken house.

"Come with me," Pa beckoned, as we walked to the homemade tractor parked under an oak tree that had turned a beautiful shade of reddish-brown. He hopped on the seat, pulled on the choke wire, pushed the starter button, and the engine caught the first time. Then he slid to the ground.

"Here," he said. "You drive. You're old enough to steer this thing while we pick up potato boxes."

"But how do I start moving?"

"Just push in the clutch, slip the shifting lever into dual low, put your other foot on the gas pedal, slowly let out the clutch, and push a little on the gas at the same time."

Sounded easy enough. I pushed in the clutch. I'd done this many times before, when I was play driving, so I knew how. I pulled on the lever and shifted into dual low. This I had also practiced before. Now I pushed on the gas pedal, and the engine roared a little and the machine began to vibrate. I pushed on the gas pedal some more.

"Not too much gas," Pa cautioned. He stood just back of me, on the tongue of the wagon. Slowly I let out the clutch, momentarily forgetting that my other foot continued to push on the gas pedal. With a mighty lurch, the tractor jumped forward, nearly tossing my father off his perch.

"Take your foot off the gas! Take your foot off the gas!" he yelled. I eased up on the gas pedal, and we moved slowly along the field. I was driving. By myself. For real. When we got to the end of the field, Pa showed me how to make a wide turn with the wagon, so the tractor's big rear tires wouldn't run into the front wheel of the wagon and break the wooden tongue. This I did without incident. I pushed in the clutch, shifted the lever into neutral, and jumped off the seat. A big smile spread across my face, and I felt a great sense of accomplishment. I heard people talking about feeling like a man. This was surely what it was like. Being a man was a fine feeling.

"You're not done yet," Pa said. "Drive back across the field while Weston and I load these potato boxes on the wagon. Stop when I tell you to."

This time I did better with the clutch and gas pedal, and the tractor began moving along the soft potato ground. I stopped by the first several potato boxes while Weston and Pa promptly loaded them onto the wagon. Then I drove on. It was going well, exceedingly well. What was so complicated about driving a tractor, I wondered? Why all the fuss? There was nothing to it. A little steering to avoid running over the potato boxes and the potato plants not yet dug, a little thinking about how to let out the clutch and push down on the gas pedal at the same time, and listening to Pa say when I should stop and start. After two or three stops and starts, I had it down pat. I sat up straight on the tractor seat, hoping someone like maybe Jim Kolka would pass by on the road and see me driving the tractor. Kolkas didn't have a tractor—not a homemade one, not a factory-made one. Nothing. They depended for all their pulling on a pair of buckskin-colored draft horses, a rather tired pair that plodded along in a truly unspectacular way. What a great thing it would be if Jim or one of the other neighbor kids saw me driving this shiny new tractor, even if it wasn't factory built and didn't have the name John Deere or McCormick-Deering or Fordson stamped on it. Model A Ford was good enough for me. Besides, everybody knew what a Model A Ford was. Several neighbors had Model A Ford cars and they swore by them, at them sometimes too, when they wouldn't start.

I approached the top of a rather steep hill. I stopped while Pa and Weston lifted several more potato boxes on the wagon, then I eased ahead, not quite sure how I should stop mid-hill. Stop I surely must for four or five filled potato boxes sat waiting half-way down the slope. Slowly I eased forward, the tractor gears holding the load back and making driving easier.

"Whoa!" Pa yelled. Much later, when we no longer had horses on the farm, he still yelled "Whoa!" when he meant stop.

I confidently pushed in the clutch and, rather than stop, the tractor began gaining speed.

"Push on the brake!" Pa yelled. I'd practiced this earlier but when the tractor was standing still. I pushed as hard as I could but nothing happened. The tractor with the partially loaded wagon of filled potato boxes moved even faster.

"Push on the brake!" Pa yelled again with some concern in his voice. I began staring at the brake pedal and my foot that somehow wasn't accomplishing the right thing. Glancing down was a major mistake.

"Look out for the potato boxes!" Pa yelled.

I looked up to see the right front tractor wheel hit the first wooden box dead center. I heard a sickening, splintering sound as the wood broke. I saw potatoes rolling down the hill. Then, before I could recover, I hit the next box, and the next, and the next, and somehow missed the last one on the hillside. At the bottom of the hill, I let out the clutch and killed the engine. I put my hands over my face, expecting the worst, when Pa caught up with the runaway rig.

"You hurt?" he asked, out of breath.

"Nah," I answered. "Smashed some boxes, didn't I?" The obvious was all I could think to say.

"Yup. Hop down and help Weston and me pick up the spilled potatoes and the kindling wood."

That's all he said. No punishment. No tongue lashing. Later, he showed me how to brace myself on the seat so I could get more leverage out of my right leg and push the brake far enough to stop the tractor. He also reminded me that had I gently let out the clutch, the tractor would also have stopped.

As I think about it now, I learned a lot more than a valuable driving lesson that day. I learned I shouldn't become confident too quickly when doing something new like driving a tractor. And I gained a new respect for Pa, too. By the end of the potato season, I was driving our shiny new tractor everywhere.

Doodlebug Tractor

A dapper-looking farm couple stand proudly alongside their homemade doodlebug tractor built from a Ford automobile.

ME-GO CONVERTIBLE TRACTOR ATTACHMENT

utilizes power at two opposite sides of wheel—one pushes, the other pulls, thus equalizing the strain. With this distribution of applied power there is no one point that performs all the work. No single pinion carries the total load. The power is distributed equally thru our entire system of enmeshed gears, and no single parts are wearing out thru overwork.

See Our Exhibit and Demonstrations at Minnesota State Fair.

Price $250 F. O. B. Twin Cities.

State and local distributors wanted.

CONVERTIBLE TRACTOR CORP.

1485-1487-1489 Marshall Ave.   ST. PAUL, MINN.

(PATENTED)

Another Dream Fulfilled

BY PATRICIA PENTON LEIMBACH

Patricia Penton Leimbach is farming's Erma Bombeck. Like Bombeck, she is a sage philosopher on the trials and tribulations of everyday life. She writes with a sharp pen about the joys and troubles, the hard work and humor, the meaning and value of rural living.

Leimbach was raised on a fruit farm near Lorain, Ohio. Alongside her, now-late, husband Paul, a fourth-generation farmer, she has run End o' Way farm in Vermilion, Ohio, for more than four decades.

It is through her writing that Leimbach has become one of the best known farm women in North America. For many years, she authored the weekly "Country Wife" column in the Elyria, Ohio, *Chronicle Telegram* newspaper. She also has three books to her credit, *A Thread of Blue Denim*, *All My Meadows*, and *Harvest of Bittersweet*, all of which are filled with wit and wisdom culled from her firsthand knowledge of everything from raising puppies to driving truck. In this essay, she celebrates the arrival of yet another tractor.

Here comes your new tractor," said Paul, looking up from lunch and down the road in response to the dogs' barking.

"If it's all the same to you, I'd just as soon have a Mercedes Benz," I said, looking out to where the International dealer was passing in a red blur.

The timing couldn't have been worse. I had come home late for lunch from running errands in town to find Paul cooking a couple of hot dogs (a sure sign of a farm wife's failure). As I heaved a half-bushel of canning tomatoes up onto the counter by the sink, he started carping at me about some grievances that had nothing to do with me.

"Honey, if you're angry with the guy, go tell him. Don't take it out on me!"

It evolved that the mailman had arrived just ahead of me and the implement dealer with a tardy check from the commission house. Some of the melon receipts as reflected in the check hadn't covered the cost of the boxes we packed the melons in. And now came this big new liability.

Whether I'm to hold title to "my tractor" or just pay for it had not as yet been determined, but my perambulations among farm people have taught me that a growing number of farm wives are working at outside jobs to keep the machinery from being repossessed. I pulled on my barn coat and went out to where the implement dealer had just unloaded the thing.

Shiny and red it was, and so clean! Hard to imagine this showroom model up to its axles in mud and manure. Not difficult, however, to imagine the pride of a farmer riding thereon. And a farmer's wife could cut quite a figure up there too on that adjustable, padded seat—with arms, no less. Wow!

"Well," I said sarcastically, not quite ready to surrender to this folly, "it's the right color, no doubt about that. But it doesn't have my name painted on it anyplace. And does it go with all that stuff out there that it's supposed to pull?"

A new tractor is like a new suit. The shirt and the tie, the hat and the shoes have to match—likewise, the plow, the cultivator, the front end loader, the mower, and so on. Paul assured me that this tractor would fit well into our "machinery wardrobe."

The International dealer got on it then and demonstrated how the front end loader could be simply removed by slipping the cotter pins and pulling a couple of bolts.

"There's something you should appreciate," said Paul, making veiled reference to a skirmish I once had with a tree that was camouflaged in Virginia creeper. I bent the old bucket all to heck.

" . . . and see here, Pat, it's got a Bosch carburetor—just like a Mercedes-Benz," we finished in unison, laughing.

Someplace toward the end of her second or third decade as a farm wife, every woman must wake up one morning, look wistfully out toward the tractors in the machinery lot, and say to herself, "Is this all there is?"

Of course it isn't! There are new pickups, new plows, new planters, new discs; augers, manure spreaders, sprayers, chisel plows, wagons, and if you are very zealous and faithful, one golden summer day you'll get a shiny new combine!

And when Fred dies and leaves you a wealthy widow, all the eligible old duffers in the county will come around and size up your machinery lot. Just make sure it's all in your name.

At the Controls

Ma poses proudly at wheel of the family Case.

Pa watches as Junior and Spot pretend to be driving the family's Deere in this famous advertising painting by artist Walter Haskell Hinton.

MASSEY-HARRIS

TWIN=POWER 101 TRACTOR ☆

Pa shows Sis how to drive the family Massey-Harris Model 101.

Old Farmer

BY KIM PRATT

Kim Pratt is a writer and editor for *Yesterday's Tractors*, an online antique tractor magazine and resource website. The site includes everything from historical research to how-to advice as well as poems and essays about life with tractors.

"Old Farmer," a.k.a. Dale Jensen, began posting his recollections for *Yesterday's Tractors* when he was at the grand age of 75. With an extensive knowledge of farming and tractors, he valued the past and the ways that went with it. He shared these values with the website readers until shortly before his passing. The following recollections are culled from Old Farmer's essays.

THE DAY THE TRACTOR STOOD STILL

Today I thought it would be a nice day to go out and putt around on my old John Deere G. I went out to the barn, slid the door open, and there she was. I went up and turned the fuel on, then pulled the throttle ahead some. I opened the petcocks, choked it, spun the flywheel twice. Then I shut the choke off, spun the flywheel and spun it and spun it until finally, half dead and out of breath, I was able to mutter some words I can't repeat here.

I was ready for another round, so I tried to start it again. It still wouldn't start so I laid in the straw of the barn floor, out of breath, and muttered some more words that I can't repeat. I then thought that maybe I had a dirty fuel system. So I opened the gas lid and it was bone dry. I almost killed myself: there was no gas in it! So I put gas in it and spun the wheel a bit. She fired right up. Boy, did I feel dumb.

I need to paint on all of my tractors: "Check gas before starting." I guess it's just age.

JOHN DEERE MAN

I was born November 19, 1923, and was raised on a farm in southeastern South Dakota. I was born in a time when horses still worked the land and tractors were new. I was raised on hard work and in a big family; we had good times and bad times, but mostly good. My first tractor was a beat-up Farmall F-12. I went to World War II, came home, traded the Farmall for a John Deere Model A, and took over the family farm. I've been a John Deere man ever since.

CONVERSION TO THE TRACTOR

I suppose none of you guys ever farmed with horses, but I was just a kid and remember when we did it. What a pain! Those old horses would bite and everything else. Our neighbor had a big old Case steam engine and I was amazed seeing it pull a ten-bottom plow. Well, we pulled our single plow with horses. Our other neighbor had a Waterloo Boy, and he thought it was the best thing around.

I was angry that we didn't have a tractor until one day I came home and I saw a John Deere Model GP in front of the barn popping. I was so happy I about cried. Dad kept the team of horses, though. He really liked them, and they could help with the work. We had the GP until 1937 when we traded it for the John Deere Model G, which I still have.

Our neighbors all got John Deere Model As after seeing how good our two-cylinder was. The neighbor's old Case steam engine was cut up during World War II. The metal scrappers took her away from the place and his Waterloo Boy served as a backup tractor until about 1949.

MEMORIES OF THE FARM

Do you remember when you were a kid on the farm, all the stuff you got yelled at for? I remember some—like when we had the John Deere G, Dad would tell me to keep it in low when I drove home. Well, one night I decided to be a speed racer and put it in full throttle. I put my foot on the governor, and boy, I thought I was sure moving along.

I was going down the road and thought I might be home before it got real dark when from over the hill came a pair of headlights and they were going fast! I tried to pull the clutch back to stop the tractor but I couldn't pull it back. Then it came by me, it was our neighbor's boy in his Model A roadster. He was taking the whole road, so my only choice was the ditch.

Down I went, through the fence and right into the hay field. I pulled the throttle back, slammed both brakes on, and used both hands to pull the clutch back. Dad sure was mad!

I also remember discing by the house. Dad would come out and say, "Quit lugging that thing around. If you don't know how to drive it, get off!" But I knew if I got off the tractor it would only make him angry. It seems like I was always in trouble.

I was either playing in the creek or catching chickens or chasing the pigs. I never understood why Dad would be so angry. But when I got my own kids, I finally figured it out. He was just trying to look out for us—that's why he would tell me to stay away from that picker or watch out on that tractor. He was just trying to watch out for me, not trying to make my life miserable

THE DEMISE OF A FAMILY FARM

I bought an old family farm back in 1974, about a year after I bought the eighty acres around it. I was just starting to get big in farming, and my brother and I were buying up all kinds of land. The farm I bought was the farm where my best friend grew up as a kid. They use to come over to our house and help with the farm work a lot.

The other day my son parked his payloader at that old place we got and he told me he's pushing the place down but its been raining today so he couldn't do it. So I went and took a last look at the farm. I walked into the barn and felt a eerie feeling...I got chills as I could hear the old John Deere at work and the cows in the barn. I looked around and found an old pitchfork, probably the one we used to pitch bundles when we threshed. There was a lot of old stuff in there. I moved on to the old grainery where I found an old corn sheller and the beat-up grill from a Farmall M.

Next I went to the feed shed were I found old tools and gauges from an old Dodge Brothers car or truck. The chicken shed had collapsed and I could see the twisted pieces of tin that were once feeders for chickens. The hog house was still in good shape but the lightning rods had been shot. Then there was the small tin shed falling down where they kept the tractors. I went in and saw an old John Deere jack and a rusty back wheel from an M or H Farmall. The old workbench still had old parts on it. I then looked in the trees where I found the remains of a New Idea manure spreader and a 101 picker. Behind the barn sat an old Model T frame.

I went back to my truck and drove home. I started thinking about that place, how the family farms are going away because of selfish farmers like me buying up all their land. If I could do it over again I don't think I ever would have gone big.

When I looked through that farm and saw all the stuff, I remembered all the small farms having old junk around. It was a way of life. Now, the big farms have new homes and big Morton buildings. But that's not the way it was back then. We all built the barn or the hog house together, everybody just farmed a small piece and that was plenty. To me it was a simpler way of life.

REGRETS?

You know I've been farming for years and I got to thinking, was it all a waste? What did I gain? It's all a gamble, and sometimes you lose money. Like now, this year, we got acres of corn—and I mean acres!—and prices are down and there's no place for it to go. It seems like I should have done something else like be a mechanic on tractors or opened a tractor dealership or something. Instead I busted my back pulling out rocks and stumps to try to clear land to farm and turned it into a big farm that has so much land I don't have any money to farm it. I tell my brothers that we should get rid of our 8,400 acres, stop renting some land, and become a bit smaller. But they won't listen. It's all going to come back and haunt us some day that we killed small farms.

I wish I still had a small farm. I remember that everybody farmed a small piece, had a tractor, some chickens, ten hogs, and fifteen cows. That was a family farm. When I think about it, it's like the ending of a poem I read yesterday: "we must keep with the times." You know sometimes I wonder if it was all for nothing. Did I do the right thing? Should I have been a doctor instead? Sometimes I wonder and my only answer is, I don't know.

Well, there is no going back now. I made up my mind back in the 1940s and I can't change that. But still I wonder, if I would have been a tractor mechanic would I be where I am now? If I were a doctor would I be rich now? I don't know but I think I made the right choice. I have a good family and that's probably all I really need.

SAYING GOODBYE

This morning I woke up and instead of sitting in the house all day like I have been, I got my bibs on and my seed-corn cap and I walked out the door to the barnyard like I have done so many times before. I walked toward the barn and managed to slide the old rotten door open, and there she was: the words "John Deere" could be easily seen through the dark light of the barn. I walked up to it, turned the gas on and opened the petcocks like so many other mornings. But this time I couldn't start the old G. My grandson had to do it for me. He gave her two whirls and she popped and then a good yank and she came to life. She sat there at idle like she had done so many times before.

The familiar pop-pop brought me back to the days of my youth. I climbed onto the seat of the once-huge tractor and took it out of the barn. I drove it out back, and my grandson hooked the old disc up to it. I was off discing.

The old G was working under a load with me again, perhaps the last load with me as the driver. We disced for what seemed forever; I just thought about my life the whole time and just listened to the old G sing its song. The popping of a two-banger is one of the most beautiful sounds I have ever heard. I got done and drove her back to the shed. I backed it in, shut the gas off, throttled it down, and listened until its last pop had died out, like it was saying goodbye.

I slid the door shut and walked back to the house. I thought about the old G and it's last load, and how the G and I will be apart not long from now. I guess it was like kind of saying goodbye to an old friend.

FINAL NOTE: THE LAST HARVEST

In August of 1999, Old Farmer told his many online friends that he wasn't feeling well and knew he didn't have much longer to live. He said he was ready to pass on, but prayed he could at least live long enough to see the last harvest. His prayers were answered, and in early October he was out helping his family in the field. His final moments came when he went to get the John Deere 3010 as his son got the combine. Old Farmer passed away on the seat of that tractor and was found later by his son with the engine still running. He was able to see some of the harvest he had spoke of so often. Buried in his old seed-corn cap, a twenty-one-gun salute was performed at the cemetery in honor of his service in World War II.

Saying "So Long" to an Old Friend on the Farm

BY FRITZ NORDENGREN

Fritz Nordengren writes about small farms, sustainable farming practices, and the good life on his blog, *Small Farm Life*. His Two Mile Ranch is situated deep in the heart of Iowa.

It is time this week to say good bye to my first friend at Two Mile Ranch. That friend is Ol Red, the Farmall 706 that came as part of the property deal when I bought the farm in 2005.

I never called "Ol Red" by name except in this blog. A tractor does not have the anthropomorphic qualities of the clever creations by Disney and Pixar. A tractor is a tool, a 50-horsepower piece of iron that when used, taught me valuable lessons.

The previous owners of the farm assured me the tractor was in great shape—if I wanted to buy it on top of our land purchase. Once I insisted it be part of the transaction, it was suddenly "as-is." The right front tire was flat. It did not start. So my Realtor and Norman, my neighbor, and I put on a new battery, drained the gasoline-turned-sludge out of the fuel line, and while we could start it, it wouldn't run until I replaced a solenoid wire.

That first spring, I learned my first real safety lesson about tractors. With kids in the cab (never again) I slid on wet grass and became high centered in a gully wash. God looked over us that day...the outcome could have been much worse.

As a result, we met Virlin and Brenda, neighbors who now watch over my daughter's horse. Good people, they pulled us out of the gully. The right front tire was off the rim, and because of that, I met Bob of Bob's Barn, where many of us meet on Saturday mornings to talk about life, the weather, government, and all that is great about sitting at Bob's Barn, talking about the above, instead of actually doing work. This Saturday was no different, except Bob was hard at work on a tractor, moving the wide set rear wheels in to accommodate a narrower track cultivator. The rest of us stood around watching him work. It almost looked like some odd, faith-healing ritual. Frosty, the oldest of the group, offered up a tip on how to move the tires in using a long chain. Very impressive. You can learn a lot from these guys if you just watch and listen.

That first year, I spent a lot of time mowing down the overgrowth trying to learn the shape and lay of the land. A friend of mine, a long time farmer, did the first pass of mowing for me through the tall waist- and shoulder-high grass, helping see places I could safely take the tractor.

The following year, Bob led me to a 12-foot disc about 30 miles from here. I towed it home with my pickup at about 20 miles per hour and that spring was able to strip disc part of the pheasant habitat in CRP. I also spent more time mowing.

Then in 2007 and 2008 I disced and planted food plots. Long hours in a tractor, but nothing like the fulltime farmers who spend marathon days working their soils.

My most impressive feat was towing a lumber yard delivery truck out of the mud after he became stuck. I say my feat, but I didn't do much more than sit behind the wheel and let out the clutch, the mighty IH Farmall engine did the real work, and I got the glory.

This year, the last time I used it for work, I used a borrowed blade to move a pile of manure across my soon to be planted garden. I think I'll remember that spring day the longest.

The memory includes another friend who I've said "so long" to as well. "King Louie"—the pheasant who thought he was a dog—insisted on charging at the tractor and running beneath its wheels as I worked. I had to stop several times and chase him off to be sure I didn't run him over. He hung around the farm a few more weeks, and after nesting season began, he disappeared.

Which brings us to last week and Sunday. A new potential owner for the Farmall stopped by. He had heard I was selling the tractor and is building a campground nearby and it would be a good match. My needs are now for a smaller tractor; a "chore" tractor that can do some mowing, some loader work, and drink less gas.

Today, he and another man came by and negotiated a tough, but fair deal for both of us. He'll pick it up early in the week and I say "so long" to an old friend. It's a great tractor with lots of life in it. In a Pixar movie, "retiring" to a campground sounds like a plot device. In the real world of Two Mile Ranch, it's time to go tractor shopping.

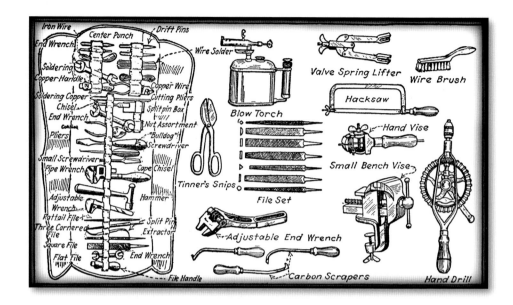

Iron Wire · Center Punch · Drift Pins · Wire Solder · Valve Spring Lifter · Wire Brush · End Wrench · Soldering Copper Handle · Copper Wire · Cutting Pliers · Blow Torch · Hacksaw · Soldering Copper Chisel · Split pin Box · Nut Assortment · Hand Vise · End Wrench · "Bulldog" Screwdriver · Pliers · Small Bench Vise · Small Screwdriver · Pipe Wrench · Cape Chisel · Tinner's Snips · File Set · Adjustable Wrench · Hammer · Rattail File · Three Cornered File · Split Pin Extractor · Adjustable End Wrench · Square File · Flat File · End Wrench · File Handle · Carbon Scrapers · Hand Drill

History in the Barn

BY MICHAEL DREGNI

It was while doing the morning chores that we came upon the tractor in the barn. I was tagging along with my friend, David Benson, helping him with his chores, but more often than not simply chatting and gabbing as he played the tour guide, showing off his eclectic collection of machinery as we made the rounds of his farm in southwestern Minnesota. It was a typical autumn day in that part of the country—which is to say, the kind of glorious, clear, cool, sunny day that made farmwork a joy.

Now, my friend's farm was not your typical farm. There was not your usual modern Ford or Kubota tractor parked in the machine shed, nor your Ford and Chevrolet pickup truck pulled up in front of the house.

Things operated different here.

My friend's farm led a secret second life as a kind of orphanage for mechanical foundlings, a safe house for wayward technology, a retirement home for obsolete engineering, and a last resort for unwanted machinery. And the farm was surrounded by windbreaks that protected the home place from the westerly winds, but also served as a graveyard for old tractors, trucks, and implements that seemed to not truly be dead but simply waiting to be resurrected once again.

Let me explain further.

In the barn, next to a handful of dairy cows, were stables for two Percheron workhorses. And these gentle giants, a mother and her daughter, still worked, pulling manure spreaders, hay wagons, and a rock-gathering flatbed in the fields. A small herd of sheep, a gaggle of geese, and a flock of chickens lived in other outbuildings, sheds, and henhouses. With the mix of crops, this seemed like your typical 1930s family farm—albeit transported by a time machine smack dab into the 1990s.

But it was the choice of machinery that truly set my friend's farm apart. The son of Swedish immigrants, who at that time still lived on the homeplace, my friend had inherited a love and fascination for equipment that originated from far-flung shores.

With his Swedish heritage it should come as little shock that he was enamored with Volvo automobiles. Yet this love affair with the Swedish car went beyond simple transportation needs. On the farm at any one time may be a gaggle of Volvo sedans, coupes, and sports cars ranging in vintage over a spectrum of four decades of age from the 1950s through the 1980s. The favored setup was naturally Volvo's famous station wagon, which due to its heavy-duty clutch and shock absorbers, capable chassis, high-output heater, and huge wagon bed, made it ideal to serve double duty in the farm's fields for walking soybeans, picking rocks, mending fences, and any other sundry chore. The only thing the station wagons lacked in comparison with your typical Ford pickup truck was four-wheel drive.

Now it might seem odd to use a fleet of Volvo station wagons as general-purpose farm pickup trucks—sort of like using a goat for a lawn mower. But when you reconsidered, Willys' Jeep and the Land-Rover were offered after World War II with plows and other specially built farm implements, so why not? If my friend chose Volvo station wagons instead of the tried-and-true Ford or Chevy pickup truck, well, that was his choice.

The thing is, those Volvos shared valuable machinery shed space with a virtual museum of ancient motorcycles. On first glance, these cycles seemed to be collected and curated to display the complex variety of cycles that were created in all corners of the globe. But as you made the rounds with my friend and heard each cycle's story, you understood that there was meaning to their existence on the farm. A duo of 1960s

Triumph vertical twins, for instance, had a favored place in a shed, as they also shared a favored place in my friend's memory: He had bought these cycles with an acquaintance in England during a college-years grand tour of Europe. The Triumphs came home with them and served time on the farm for everything from herding stock to quick-and-dirty gofer transportation.

Near the Triumphs was parked an English-built Ariel single; other American and European steeds stood in the shadows, too covered by the dust of the years to differentiate the brands without the aid of a cleaning rag and sometimes, a magnifying glass to examine the worn decals or emblems on the tanks. Another shed contained a bevy of BMWs of different ages and configurations, which was another favored brand as a BMW R26 single had carried my friend and his soon-to-be-wife on a tour of the Baja Peninsula also during their college days. A 1950s German-made NSU 500-cc single waited out its time on this earth in a stable nearby, while my friend shook his head over a rare Velocette thumper that he had just missed out on at a neighboring farm auction. He probably had plans to pull stumps with it or something.

But it was in the wide and varied selection of farm tractors that my friend truly excelled. The casual observer practically needed a pocket-sized field guide to tractors to keep tabs on the variety of machines as you strolled the acreage. Fortunately, I had my friend as tour guide on this fine fall morning.

We walked by a John Deere Model A that was waiting patiently in the center of the farmyard to do its chores. The choice of a Johnny Popper was nothing out of the ordinary, but its vintage and story were: My friend's dad had bought this A brand new in 1951 and used it throughout his farming career; my friend still had it and used it regularly. This was no coddled and polished showpiece—although after its lifetime of hard farm labor, it probably deserved to be.

The Model A shared chores with two other green machines bearing the yellow deer insignia: a 1939 Model B and a 1949 Model R. The R had been purchased from a retired neighbor, who had bought the diesel new; his daughter now was interested in buying it back as she had fond memories of plowing with her dad's old Deere. Another Model R hibernated behind some outbuildings, where it donated its components as a parts tractor to keep the '49 R alive and well.

My friend's favored mounts—at the moment at least—were two David Brown tractors, which hailed from Great Britain. The David Brown concern's history stretched back to 1860 when it made gears for early mechanical contrivances. In 1936, Brown joined forced with Irishman Harry Ferguson to build their short-lived Ferguson-Brown Model A. Ferguson soon left for greener pastures and a handshake agreement with Henry Ford to produce the famed Ford-Ferguson N Series. Brown soldiered on with tractors of his own, which became cousins to another of Brown's ventures: hand-crafting the glorious Aston Martin and Lagonda automobiles. The machines that had somehow immigrated to this Minnesota farmstead were a 1960s Model 880 and 990; a third David Brown slumbered in the windbreak.

Sharing a shed with the David Browns were two 1970s Deutz air-cooled diesel tractors, which were growing in popularity on this farm at the moment. These machines hailed from Germany, where the Deutz firm boasted a proud history. In 1907, Deutz was the pioneer builder of tractors powered by the fledgling four-cycle internal-combustion engine. Deutz's Pfuglokomotive, or "Plow-locomotive," was a massive 3-ton affair featuring a 25-horsepower gas-fueled engine.

In addition to the working machines, a mishmash of obsolete but ageless iron rested their bones in the windbreak, ancient American machines that were built by farsighted entrepreneurs in the early days of the tractor. The names cast into the radiators were grown over by the prairie grasses, grasses that these tractors had once turned over while breaking the virgin land. Trees—some of them perhaps two decades old—had grown up through open areas of the tractor chassis.

Now, this was far more horsepower than a small family farm required, but obviously that was not the point of having all of these tractors and other machines. My friend harbored a fascination for these machines that transcended the need to plant oats and cut hay.

Thus, it should have come as little surprise to me on this beautiful fall day when we came upon yet another tractor in yet another barn.

This tractor, however, was truly special. It sat in a far-flung shed that had once held animal stables but now was filled with all of the other unrecognizable and incomplete bits of machinery that a farm accumulates over the years. The tractor was lost in the shadows of the small barn but as we entered, light from the doorway cast a golden glow over the old

machine that to any lover of old machines would have been indistin-
guishable from a halo. My friend simply stood in the doorway, regarding
this last tractor fondly and allowing me a moment of discovery.

I walked into the barn as if I was walking into a sepulcher, stirring
up motes of dust and dry hay with each footstep. I moved around the
cobweb-covered tractor with reverence, not daring to touch it.

The tractor was a John Deere D. It was a 1927 model, as my friend
told me.

For some reason, we were speaking with almost hushed voices.

I continued to circle the machine, admiring its straightforward
design, a design that was purely functional with none of the streamlin-
ing that Henry Dreyfuss would later add to the Deeres. The wheels were
bare iron cleats and the seat was a solid cast saddle. This was a machine
for working.

As any tractor enthusiast worth his or her salt knows, the Model
D is one of the most famous farm tractors ever. The D also holds the
record for the longest production run of any American tractor, being
built from 1923 to 1953—a thirty-year run that is challenged only by
Farmall's Cub at twenty-eight years. The D was the first tractor on many
an American farm, the mechanical mule that replaced the horses, the
machine that broke the prairie sod, the tractor that helped provide food
for a growing nation. During its day, some 160,000 Model D tractors were
built, a testament to its capabilities and the respect farmers held for this
simple machine.

What's this D's history, I asked, sort of like one would ask after the
bloodlines of a thoroughbred race horse.

My friend had also fallen under the spell of the tractor and so it was
a moment before he could shift gears to relate the story.

It was the autumn of 1966, and my friend was working at the tractor salvageyard south of Worthington, Minnesota, saving money to go
off to college. This salvageyard was one of the largest anywhere. It bore
a collection of tractors, implements, and combines that were sorted by
color—and hence by make—into rows that stretched away to the horizon, undulating over the rolling hillsides. From the distance, the salvageyard glowed like fields of some rare, beautiful flowers: a section of red
tulips, maybe; another of bright green neighboring patches of gold, light
blue, orange, and more. Yet the red was Farmall Red, the green was Deere

Green, the gold was Minneapolis-Moline's trademark Prairie Gold, the blue was Ford Blue, the orange Case's Flambeau Red—every color farm tractors were ever painted. At sunset, with the prairie light reflecting off of the ancient sheetmetal, it was truly a gorgeous sight.

My friend was finishing up his employment at the yard before leaving for college when one day this 1927 Deere Model D appeared. It was complete, which was a rare thing for a tractor this old. It had been hauled in from a farm somewhere in Nebraska, just one more piece of obsolete machinery. By chance or by luck, this D had not been melted down as part of the scrap metal drive during World War II. Now, in 1966, however, it was really too old to add to the salvageyard inventory: No one was still using such an ancient machine and would ever want parts. So, this D was destined to be junked out.

My friend caught sight of the D and something about this decades-old piece of farming history spoke to him, a teenager. He hustled in to talk to the owner of the salvageyard and begged him not to junk out the tractor. The owner may have sensed the history of this particular machine, but old tractors were just old tractors in the 1960s and business was always business. The machine was going to be junked.

My friend thought quick. He offered a bargain: He would work to buy the D. And so a deal was struck. My friend labored an extra week for no pay and when the week was up, the old D was his.

He got the D home to his parents' farm, parked it in the barn, and left for college. The D had sat here ever since.

Now, twenty-some years later, we both stood silently for a while, staring at the tractor. I suppose he was thinking of old days and the way things once were. I was mesmerized by the story: A youth on his way to college and a tractor that was saved from the dustbins of history. But it was even more than that: This tractor was history itself.

After we had gotten our fill of gazing at the venerable old D, we gathered up our gear and got ready to set off doing chores again. But there was one chore still to do in this barn, part of my friend's typical rounds. Many of the cars, cycles, and tractors on his farm he used—if not daily, well, at least once a month or so. Other machines he just let sit. Some he had good intentions or dreams of getting around to fixing while their parts rusted as solid as the original lump of iron ore from which they were made. A single person simply couldn't get keep all of these machines among the living. But the D was special, something separate and apart from all of the other machines on the farm. And this gave it a place in his chores, along with feeding the chickens, tending to the draft-horses, and milking the cows. Whenever his farm work brought him by this barn, he stopped for a moment, open the old doors, went inside to the D, and grasped its solid flywheel with both of his hands, leaned into it with his weight, and turned the flywheel so that the D's crankshaft and rods and pistons and all of the rest of its engine would never seize up.

38204000019564